D1243039

Black
Pentecostalism

Southern Religion in an
Urban World

Arthur E. Paris

The University of Massachusetts Press
Amherst, 1982

*This book is dedicated to: my parents and grandparents,
who encouraged and sustained me
as I set my feet on a scholar's path*

The publisher acknowledges permission granted to reprint
selections from the following material: G. Norman Eddy,
"Store-Front Religion," *Religion in Life* 28 (1958–59); Charles
S. Johnson, *The Shadow of the Plantation,* by permission of
The University of Chicago Press, copyright 1934 by The
University of Chicago; Albert Raboteau, *Slave Religion,* by
permission of Oxford University Press, copyright © 1978 by
Oxford University Press, Inc.; Vinson Synan, *The Holiness-
Pentecostal Movement in the United States* (Grand Rapids,
1971), by permission of W. B. Eerdmans Publishing Company.

Contents

Acknowledgments

Like most authors, I have contracted a wide range of debts: to former teachers, to fellow scholars, and especially to the people who are the subjects of this inquiry. It is of course impossible to acknowledge them all; space does not permit it, and memory will doubtless fail at several crucial names. Hence it seemed better to keep these notations as brief as practicable. Therefore let me give credit to those who structured my interests in these matters, especially Marlis Kreuger, Howard S. Becker, and Remi Clignet. They helped shape my perspectives and guided my inquiries. Professors Robin Williams, Pharnel Longus, and Paget Henry were among the many who read and made helpful comments about various sections of the manuscript. John Szwed (and NIMH) helped make the field work possible with a fellowship from the Institute of Urban Ethnography at the University of Pennsylvania. The Rev. Benny and Mary Goodwin introduced me to the people of Mount Calvary and I suppose bear some ultimate responsibility for my intense interest in this church. They also encouraged me when the going was rough and, along with my editor, Dick Martin, helped sustain my efforts when energies and interests flagged.

Most of the credit for the ultimate success of my inquiry, however, rests with the members of the Boston congregations, who "gave me a church home," and answered my seemingly endless queries with patience and good humor. Of course as with all such works, responsibility for any errors rests solely with me.

Preface

This book is the culmination of a project of rather lengthy gestation. It grew out of a general and long-standing concern with Black religion and specifically with the religious expression of the Black lower classes. The conventional wisdom in regard to lower-class Black religion has fastened on surface appearances and superficial characteristics. Too often, both the popular mind and the social science literature have seemed to miss the point, focusing, for example, on the enthusiasm associated with lower-class Black religious expression while treating that expression with condescension and a lack of understanding and viewing it as inferior to the "normative" practice of mainline White denominations. It has often been noted that the Black ghetto is "overchurched"; the "excessive" number of churches in lower-class Black neighborhoods being regarded as a sign of waste and religious mismanagement. Too many churches and too many preachers vying for the support of the lower-class population lead inevitably to a waste of energy and resources. There ensues a constant struggle for survival among congregations with too few members to maintain adequate levels of support. Fewer congregations would mean greater levels of support for those remaining and would lower the financial burdens imposed on individual members. The numerous "storefront" churches of this segment of the population exemplify these tendencies and are responsible for encouraging some of this condescending analysis.

This work looks at several Black lower-class churches in an

attempt both to understand them and to critically evaluate the categories previously used to analyze them.

To this end, the author undertook a participant observation study of three Boston congregations of the Mount Calvary Holy Church of America, Inc. The fieldwork took place over an eighteen-month period, from the fall of 1971 through the spring of 1973, during which time an attempt was also made to consider the three Mount Calvary churches in connection with other Holiness and Pentecostal churches in Boston.

This study takes explicit exception to the dominant view noted above and attempts an alternative description along three dimensions: historical, organizational, and theological. The weight of the analysis is to "normalize" the phenomenon and thereby retrieve it from the realm of the exotic or the bizarre. By giving these churches a history and pedigree, by putting them within an organizational context shared by other churches and institutions, and by locating them theologically, a more accurate picture emerges than heretofore available. Of equal importance, these churches are located within a sociohistorical context productive of internal and external comparison. Such "storefront churches" would benefit from comparison with other Black churches, as well as from comparison with White and other non-White religious organizations. The lines of theological development would then be more fruitfully understood, their organizational uniqueness or ordinariness would become clearer, and their sociology would be established on firmer ground.

A significant instance of disagreement with the dominant view, for example, was that there turned out to be no substantive category of "storefront church." Rather, a storefront existence is a common physical characteristic that many Black institutions have shared on the way to more dignified and substantial premises. The fact that all these institutions have operated out of commercial space, that is, storefronts, results from the convergence of the limited availability of church edifices (for the large number of groups seeking them) and the inability of impoverished congregations to afford those available. This is obviously not a new phenomenon. Many groups besides churches have occupied commercial space: government agencies, community organizations, cultural groups, and so on. Many of them, including churches, forsake such locations for more suitable quarters when financially able. In New York City, to cite one example, a number of former theaters have been given second careers as churches by congregations housed originally in smaller, often storefront, spaces.

A number of topics were not dealt with in this effort, among them the "emotionalism" of Pentecostal religion, the common instances of deviance from the strict standards of the church, and the various personal and political disputes that animate church life from time to time. The study, though concerned with the broader background of the Mount Calvary Holy Church, Inc., is properly a study of the three Boston congregations in their religious, organizational, and communal aspects. As such, I believe it adds significantly to the study of both American Pentecostalism and the religious life of Black Americans.

Introduction

This book is a study of the three Boston congregations of the Mount Calvary Holy Church of America, Inc. They are viewed within a particular historical and social context and are thus seen neither as aberrations nor as epiphenomenal; nor are they viewed as springing up ex nihilo. Rather, they are a product of a particular historical moment and continue to exist in a present that is in many ways hostile to these churches and their world views. This effort begins with a broad historical overview of post–Civil War American Protestantism, because this is the soil out of which churches such as Mount Calvary originally come. Black Holiness and Pentecostal movements are ultimately rooted in the post–Civil War revival movements that periodically swept the United States, and especially the South, until around 1930. These movements began within the "mainline" Protestant churches and were originally not divided by race. The revivalist tendencies were eventually treated as heretical and either were pushed out of the established churches by mainstream forces or left of their own accord to set up independent ecclesiastical structures.

The Black Holiness and Pentecostal churches generally stem from this division between mainline churches and revivalist movements, and more particularly from a subsequent division within the Holiness and Pentecostal churches themselves along the lines of race. This division (although it emerges at a slightly later point) parallels the division along racial lines that developed within southern Protestantism as a whole during the post–Civil War period. The Mount Calvary churches arose in turn as an offshoot of one of these Black Pentecostal–Holiness churches and are thus a product of that history.

A short history of the Mount Calvary Holy Church of America, Inc., follows the historical overview and the setting of the context. It is a brief account of the background and subsequent development of the national church from its founding in 1929 to its mature establishment. This account also provides basic background information about the establishment of the Boston congregations. These first two chapters provide the social and historical background against which the Boston congregations of this body are to be seen.

Chapter 3 is an involved discussion of the life of the church, with the enactment of ritual providing the basic metaphor for that life. It is in its ritual practice that the social organization of the church is clearly exemplified. An analysis of church life via this metaphor yields a picture of the social structure of the church in its own terms, rather than in an alien sociological grammar. Such a description is no less effective and, more important, is closer to the way church members themselves see the world. The ritual process is analyzed both in terms of its constituent elements and in terms of the roles through which it is enacted. The effort is not simply a dissection, however; it is a synthesis also. The ritual process as a whole is seen as a cogent example of the social construction of reality; that is, it exemplifies the way in which people act upon the world about them to create it along lines that are meaningful to them.

The basic metaphor of ritual, then, is used as the basis of a theoretical interpretation of the life of the church. Counterposed to this theoretical position is a critique, in chapter 4, of the relevant theoretical literature. Much of this is shown to be inadequate in that it does not take the beliefs of the adherents seriously and therefore explains away religion in terms of a reality other than that of the religious adherent. As a result, the world the observer postulates and within which he frames the believer's action is not the world within which the believer himself lives. It is not surprising therefore, that observers often find believers' belief and action ill fitted for the "world." Clearly, they are not sensible in the context of the world of the observer, but the question of whether they are sensible for the world of the believer too often remains unanswered. The interpretation offered herein attempts to take seriously the world view of the believer and to postulate a theoretical interpretation beginning at that point. A key tool in this effort was the phenomenological approach explicated by Peter S. Berger and Thomas H. Luckmann in *The Social Construction of Reality*. I found it to be most congenial for this purpose and thus have cast my own theoretical analysis in a phenomenological mode.

Chapter 5, "The Church as Social World," discusses aspects of church life not included in ritual practice, such as organizational and social (familial, for example) relations at both the local and the national levels. These relations and secondary events, liturgical and otherwise, together with the regular religious life of the church, tie the adherent more firmly within the church's web of affiliation and involvement. The added ties of the church as social world reinforce the adherent's commitment and faith.

Chapter 6, "The Church in the Social World," looks at these churches, not as worlds unto themselves, the implicit stance of chapter 5, but rather as organizations set within and forced to relate to the wider polities of which they are a part. In terms of both social and political impact upon the communities in which they reside, the churches' effect on those polities has been, to all appearances, insignificant. In terms of political influence, however, the conventional view (religion as opiate and functional adjustment) is inadequate for an understanding of the Boston situation. The case is more complex than the conventional wisdom allows. The problem of the church and politics is particular to the religious tradition from which these churches come. The difficulty, as I see it, is this: The framework of meaning these churches have fashioned from tradition supplies a holistic, religious *Weltanschauung* that provides no handles with which to grasp most (secular) political action (either the individual's or the church's as institution) in religiously meaningful terms. Most emphatically, it is not that these church folk are ignorant of the "world." Rather, their action within it is not viewed as meaningful in terms of their religious Weltanschauung—thus the lack of significant social and political impact by either the churches or their members upon their communities.

These various points are pulled together and summarized in chapter 7. The view that emerges from this examination is of a church (actually three congregations of a larger church body) that is a social and teleological system complete in these realms unto itself. It offers a comprehensive alternative explanation of "the way things are" and, through close interrelationships and a complex web of affiliation and observance (albeit confined mainly to the liturgical context), maintains a quasiautonomous social world. This then is the "key" to the life of the church. It needs nothing from the world except freedom to operate and potential recruits to maintain its world through social action. Potential members should be familiar with the Weltanschauung out of which these churches operate and therefore susceptible to their message and methods. By implication, therefore, the constituency of such churches is largely limited to populations of Blacks who either grew up in the South, where this world view and its attendant "style" of religious practice are widely influential, or were previously members and/or believers themselves. This reference to recruitment has a further implication for the future of the church. Either the church must "modernize" its message to appeal to Blacks who are no longer southern and/or traditional or it will face a declining population of empathetic potential members.

This book began as a doctoral thesis, and several years have passed since its presentation in that form. As the author, I now confront my own work from a distance. I am no longer in the same "place" I was then. Moreover, time has worked some changes within the churches. For these and other reasons, an epilogue has been added, not just as an update but as an attempt to knit back together my thinking, the contemporary Mount Calvary, and the Mount Calvary of a decade ago. The epilogue makes several structural points with which I had not been particularly concerned originally and considers the impact of large-scale structural forces on these churches as community institutions. It thereby extends the discussion of "The Church in the Social World" and adds another dimension to that more theoretical chapter.

ONE

Historical Background and Present Social Context

The history of Negro religion in the New World has just begun to be written, and that effort will not be pursued here.[1] Some of the essential elements of that history must be mentioned, however, to provide a context and a historical framework for the consideration of the religious and sociological issues that are dealt with herein. This history commences with the initial status of Blacks in the New World as chattel labor, torn from their original cultural frames and forced to confront a new and alien life experience as part of a group constituted mainly by the common experience of slavery. It progresses through the definition through common experience of this heterogeneous group of Africans into a common American Negro group, initially enslaved and then legally free;[2] their conversion and commitment to the religious beliefs of the wider society, whether in concert with or in separate organizations from Whites, through the various religious revival movements that swept the nation and particularly the South during the latter half of the nineteenth century; and subsequently, the large-scale changes in this pattern generated by the Great Migrations north and westward in this century.

1. See Albert J. Raboteau, *Slave Religion* (New York: Oxford University Press, 1978).
2. George Rawick, *Sundown to Sunup* (Westport, Conn.: Greenwood, 1972); Herbert Gutman, *The Black Family in Slavery and Freedom* (New York: Pantheon, 1976).

It is in the post–Civil War revival movements that the Holiness–Pentecostal movements among Negroes have their roots. The discussion of these groups in the social science literature is marred by faulty identification. Such groups among Blacks were initially labeled exotic and regarded as aberrations from the prevailing religious standards, that is, the established Protestant denominations. These Holiness–Pentecostal groups were described as "sects" or "cults," and their connections to the post–Civil War revivals as well as their significance as contemporary religious revival movements have been ignored. It is the elaboration of this initial history and the correction of the interpretation of the urban origins of these "exotic cults" that concern us in this chapter.

The contemporary shape of religious life among urban Blacks did not spring up ex nihilo; it is rooted in the prior history of this population as a rural peasantry and, before that, as slaves. Furthermore, although the present organization of religious practice and belief developed after the Civil War and Emancipation, the forms of Black religious experience were set long before.[3] The issue of the ultimate origin of American Negro religions is still involved in polemics, and the question of African survivals and the surrounding controversy can be avoided entirely herein.[4] It needs simply to be noted that the preeminence of Baptist and Methodist churches among Whites, particularly in the South, is paralleled by the predominance of these same two groups among

3. It is generally acknowledged that the slaves worshiped with their masters, as did Black freemen and Whites in the cities and towns. With the exception of the African Methodist Episcopal church (AME) and other Negro churches traceable to this source, Blacks and Whites continued to worship together until after Emancipation. Raper reports one rural Green County Baptist church with "seventy-three [Negro] members in 1866 and thirteen [as late as] 1876." Arthur F. Raper, *Preface to Peasantry* (Chapel Hill: University of North Carolina Press, 1936), p. 355.

4. E. Franklin Frazier, *The Negro in the United States* (New York: Macmillan, 1957); Melville J. Herskovits, *The Myth of the Negro Past* (Boston: Beacon Press, 1958); *Bulletin of the American Council of Learned Societies*, no. 32 (September 1941).

American Negroes and is due to the same cause: the large-scale proselytizing effort made by these two churches beginning with the Great Awakening(s) of the later eighteenth and early nineteenth centuries.[5] Waves of evangelism swept the South and the old Northwest:

It was during the heyday of their camp meetings and revivals at the beginning of the nineteenth century that patterns of religious expression were established. It was at this time that the ecstatic shouting, screaming, falling, rolling, laughing, jerking, and even barking of mass hysteria under the stress of religious enthusiasm, now most commonly regarded as characteristically Negro emotionalism, came into vogue. Likewise, during this early period, the sermon patterns of exhorting, with accompanying mannerisms, were first noted. Many of the stereotyped expressions which go to make up the common prayers may be traced to the vivid language of the early evangelists.[6]

It might be assumed that northern Blacks in this early colonial period, as city dwellers less affected by the evangelical fervor that swept the rural sections of the country, were less "ecstatic" in their religious practice. The literature on the colonial and antebellum periods makes clear that "enthusiasm" was also a vital part of Puritan and general Protestant colonial religious practice during the early years of settlement.[7] It is true, however,

---

5. "What the church is now to the Negro, the camp meeting was for whites of the same section as late as a generation ago. It was the chief social and religious event of the season, a festive occasion to some, an intensely religious experience for others. Negro slaves were allowed to attend them usually after the white people had had their session of religious enthusiasm and demonstration." Charles S. Johnson, *Shadow of the Plantation* (Chicago: University of Chicago Press, 1934), p. 151. See also Norvall Glen, "Negro Religion and Negro Status in the United States," in *Religion, Culture, and Society,* ed. L. Schneider (New York: John Wiley, 1964).

6. Johnson, *Shadow of the Plantation*, pp. 151–52.

7. See C. C. Goen, quoted in S. S. Hill, *Revivalism and Separatism in New England, 1740–1800* (New Haven: Yale University Press, 1952), for a general discussion of revivalist religion in New England. See also W. E. B. Du Bois, *The Philadelphia Negro* (New York: Schocken Books, 1967), pp. 220–21.

that there was a substantial difference between urban and rural (southern) Negroes during and after slavery, and these differences persisted down to the Great Migration of this century. In the early years of the colonies, the vast majority of Blacks, whether northern or southern, were slaves. Later, the North witnessed the rise of Black freemen due both to the decline of slavery as an institution (its economic basis had never been as firm in the North as in the South) and to the settling in northern states of Negroes who had escaped from slavery in the South. Northern Blacks were concentrated in the cities, unlike those in the South who were first agricultural laborers tied to rural plantations and then rural peasants. A significant proportion of the Negroes in the North had ties to (even roots in) wealthy families for whom they had served as retainers. They thus constituted an "elite" relative to other Black urbanites, and their position was, of course, much better than that of the mass of the enslaved southern population. In later years, these Blacks became small-scale businessmen, caterers, restaurateurs, tradesmen, craftsmen, and so on.[8] Their behavior reflected that of the wealthier Whites with whom they were or had been associated. Thus, in Boston, there arose a class of "Black Brahmins," who were long established in the city and who occupied among their fellow Blacks a social status parallel to that occupied by the "Boston Brahmins" among the Yankee aristocracy. These Black Brahmins also copied the cultural pretensions of the White upper classes and came to constitute a "Black bourgeoisie," in E. Franklin Frazier's terms —a group with bourgeois pretensions without the economic prerequisites upon which such a life-style is customarily based.[9]

8. Frazier, *Negro in the United States,* pp. 254–56. See also Du Bois *Philadelphia Negro;* cf. also Frank J. Webb, *The Garies and Their Friends* (New York: Arno Press, 1969), for a fictionalized portrayal of antebellum Black life in Philadelphia.
9. For a fictionalized treatment of the Black Brahmins, see Dorothy West, "The Living Is Easy" (Boston: Houghton Mifflin Co., 1948). See A. Meier, for a discussion of the old Atlanta elite beset by rising elements, August Meier and David Lewis, "History of the Negro Upper Class in Atlanta, Georgia, 1890–1958," *Journal of Negro Education* 28 (1959): 128–39.

The loss of religious enthusiasm among northern Whites was paralleled by the gradual divorce of these Negro elites from the folk culture identified with the rural masses. Thus, one sees the emergence of higher-status Black congregations, especially in the North—the rise of Methodist, Presbyterian, and even Episcopal congregations among these elites as opposed to the enthusiastic Baptist practice of the rural populace[10]—thus the gradual shift, in line with the higher-status denominational adherence, toward more decorous worship; the rejection of "gospel music" in favor of sober European hymns, and so on. This phenomenon parallels the adoption of White upper-class cultural pretensions.

As noted earlier, however, fervent religious observance was not unknown in the cities, and once the migrations began (at the turn of the twentieth century), the religious habits of the rural masses began to set the tone in northern urban Black communities.

The Great Migrations started prior to World War I and continued with some interruptions through the mid-1950s. They were initially prompted by the labor needs of expanding northern and midwestern industrial cities and the concomitant decay in southern agriculture. With the closing off of immigration of European and Asian populations early in the twentieth century, industry was forced to seek the labor of southern Blacks. Accordingly, Blacks left southern farms and went north to work in the expanding industries of urban areas, where they were used to man the industrial machinery for World War I production. After the war, the migrations continued, pushed along by the continued decline of southern agriculture. This decline was triggered by the impact of the boll weevil and, later, of synthetic fibers on cotton production. This was merely the trigger, however, for the southern agricultural economy had long been in trouble. The agricultural methods in use ruined the soil, which was then abandoned for new lands. The emphasis on the cash crops of cotton and tobacco hastened this destruction. In fact, agriculture in the South and Midwest had suffered a number of

10. Du Bois, *Philadelphia Negro,* chap. 12.

years of pre-Depression hard times following the First World War—a period of rising costs and declining prices for agricultural products.[11] Thus, the crash and the Depression of 1929 merely capped a process long begun for southern agriculture.

As a result of the economic disaster in agriculture, southern Blacks continued to be pulled off the land and into cities during the Depression. This stream continued as Black labor manned the nation's productive machinery during World War II. It is from this World War II migration and its postwar continuation that many of the people in the Boston churches come. They differ from the earlier migrants in that relatively few of them, at least in Boston, came from farms. The Boston residents are a product of "step-migration"; that is, they came to Boston from another city rather than directly from the land. The earliest immigrants were Black peasants who left the land in search of a better life. These later migrants, although similarly motivated, were no longer a peasantry but were already a lower or a working class with urban and industrial experience.

The migrants differed substantially from the indigenous urban Black populations, and these differences persisted because the migrants (especially after World War I) entered industrial and manual-labor jobs instead of the service occupations characteristic of Black urbanites in the nineteenth century. Because they soon vastly outnumbered the indigenous population, their cultural practices began to set the tone in Black communities. The religious practices of the new urban migrants were a product of their pasts; they brought their southern habits of mind to the city with them. Prior to World War II, these migrants had been rural residents, often farmers, tenants, and sharecroppers. It is important to bear in mind the determining effects of the southern agricultural economy (plantation life, wage slavery, and so on) upon Negro community organization and social structure. Because of the character of southern agriculture, Black peasants tended to live not in village or communal groups but in familial

11. Raper, *Preface to Peasantry*, pp. 201–22, gives a thorough discussion of factors involved in post–World War I migrations. See also Frazier, *Negro in the United States*, pp. 190–96.

isolation whence they went forth daily to tend their fields. This familial isolation, coupled with the formal and informal institutional and legal arrangements designed to keep the Negro in subjection and a state of dependency, prevented the growth of a broad-based cultural life built upon a number of indigenous institutions.[12] As a result, churches and lodges were the only suprafamilial cultural organizations.[13] There were other activities to relieve the drudgery of farm life—"Visiting is an escape for the rural family from the loneliness of the solitary lives which they live; it is a very important part of the social life of the rural community"[14]—but these did not have the organizational basis that characterized the churches and, to some extent, the lodges. As a result, an institutional basis for extrafamilial sociability and culture was limited to these two institutions. Because the lodges tended to focus their activities on burial and insurance, it was the church that provided the framework for community life in both the social and the ideological senses.[15] The churches encompassed, therefore, a full spectrum of the social activity of the population in addition to the strictly religious practice; suppers, socials, "frolics" all took place under the aegis of the church. Social welfare also, in the absence of state action, was handled primarily through the church. Further, because Negroes were barred from participation in wider politics, church politics commanded great attention. It is fair to say that the church defined the ideological limits of the community.

For those migrants who were not "fresh off the farm," this description is less applicable. This is a matter of degree, however, and southern life generally before World War II (and, to some

12. Johnson, *Shadow of the Plantation*, pp. 3–5.
13. Johnson (ibid., chap. 6) and Raper (*Preface to Peasantry*, chap. 20) both discuss the leisure life of rural Blacks and list visiting, sports, frolics, and dances. Only the churches, burial societies, and lodges, however, have an ongoing organizational basis.
14. Raper, *Preface to Peasantry*, p. 398.
15. "Next to the family, the church is the most important association in rural Negro communities. In fact, the church often defines the limits of the community, which often derives its name from the church organization." Frazier, *Negro in the United States*, p. 216.

extent, even now) was dominated by the churches, which set the ideological limits of belief in both the religious and the moral spheres and also regulated much of the cultural life of southern communities for Blacks and Whites.[16] Thus, although the range of leisure-time diversions and the opportunities for involvement were much greater in urban areas, many activities (movies and other theatrical entertainments, gambling, "juke" joints, and so on) were religiously proscribed; the fundamentalist world view that provided the religious basis for existence discouraged many other available pleasures. It should be clear that urban existence had its own implications for cultural and moral behavior that challenged the hegemony of the churches. In terms of the general struggle for ideological and cultural hegemony, Christianity had been losing ground to the forces of "secularism" since the mid-nineteenth century.[17] The same process that has to a large extent already run its course in northern and western metropolitan centers is still being worked through in the South. As a result, there are defections from the churches and the world views they propagate and objectify. Most people continue, however, to give lip service to the church, although it no longer occupies the central place in their lives and deviation from its norms and structures is much more open and probably also more widespread.[18] When the migrations began, there were few other institutions to which the migrants were attached, and the centrality of the church to Black life continued (and continues still for limited populations). The urban setting, with its

16. See S. S. Hill, *Southern Churches in Crisis* (Boston: Beacon Press, 1966), pp. 104–9, for a discussion of the wide social and cultural impact of southern churches on communal life.
17. Paul Boyer, *Urban Masses and Moral Order* (Cambridge: Harvard University Press, 1978). Joel Schwartz, "The Overturnings in the Earth: Firemen and Evangelists in Newark's Law and Order Crisis of the 1850's," in *Cities of the Garden State*, ed. J. Schwartz and D. Prosser (Dubuque, Iowa: Kendall/Hunt, 1977), pp. 17–34.
18. Cayton and Drake noted in the 1940s that "slightly more than half of Bronzeville's lower class adults claim to be members." Horace Cayton and St. Clair Drake, *Black Metropolis* (New York: Harcourt Brace & World, 1970), p. 612.

greater opportunities for diversion, has abetted the decline of the church's influence. At the same time, competition from external institutions—benevolent and hostile—has limited the sphere of the church's effective action and tended to shift the center of existence in people's lives to the wider society. Further, the normative appearance of much of urban existence puts great strain on a world view that condemned much of life outside the church as either evil or tending toward evil.[19] It is safe to say that, although the church has lost its ideological hegemony for the population as a whole, it continues to be the major voluntary institutional involvement for Blacks. Moreover, they maintain the traditional affiliations—predominantly Baptist and Methodist.

This is to get ahead of the issues of concern here, however, for it is precisely during the decay of the church's ideological hegemony that the small Holiness–Pentecostal or storefront churches have flourished in the very cities responsible for the loss of hegemony of the established churches. Although it is undoubtedly true that the recent history of "mainline" Protestantism has been a losing battle with secularism and that southern churches are now undergoing the same challenges to their cultural hegemony (White and Black churches alike have been losing this battle), the proliferation and continued "success" of small Holiness–Pentecostal churches in storefronts suggest that some elements of the church have been able to hold their own. In subsequent chapters, we will try to show how and why this is so. The following examination of the Pentecostal–Holiness

19. This problem has become increasingly acute for Black churches and also affects White churches, although under a different guise. The challenge to the churches' world view as reality is a central dynamic in the treatment of religion in Louise Meriwether, *Daddy Was a Numbers Runner* (New York: Pyramid Press, 1961). See also James Baldwin, *Go Tell It on the Mountain* (New York: Dial Press, 1963). The problem of legitimacy of the church world view is not just a difficulty of Black churches but has occupied American Protestantism generally for quite a while. The contemporary resurgence of charismatic movements on a broad scale notwithstanding, this breakdown in ontological status is only recently confronting the Black churches.

groups attempts to place them within the context of American religious history and provides the sociohistorical framework out of which the Mount Calvary Holy Church emerges.

Southern Revivalism and the Holiness Movement

As noted earlier, the shape of Black religious practice, with its emphasis on "enthusiasm" and biblical literalism, had been set long ago as a result of the evangelization of Blacks during the Methodist and Baptist revivals that began in the mid-eighteenth century. The religious practice and beliefs of Blacks and the majority of Whites were crystallized by the evangelical tradition of these early southern missionaries and circuit riders. Because Blacks and Whites were members (initially) of the same congregations, they shared the same world views. Theologically, the impetus was basically Wesleyan (although there was some Presbyterian and Calvinist influence in the revival movements).[20] In terms of practice, most southerners subscribed to the same fundamentalist code, which included strong prohibitions against alcohol, illicit sex, and worldly diversions such as card playing and gambling. These moral proscriptions were tied to a theological framework that emphasized a twofold experience (the "double cure") for the believer: first, conversion to justification and, second, Christian perfection or sanctification. In the first experience, the penitent was forgiven for his actual sins of commission, becoming a Christian but retaining a residue of sin. The remaining "inbred sin" was the result of Adam's fall and had to be dealt with by a second blessing, properly so-called. This experience purified the believer of inward sin, giving him "perfect love" toward God and man. This theological understanding was tied to a stance of vigorous evangelization and proselytization of the unsaved and rigorous moral rectitude and fervent

20. This treatment of the history of southern revivalism and religion is drawn largely from three works: Hill, *Southern Churches;* J. T. Nichol, *Pentecostalism* (New York: Harper and Row, 1966); V. Synan, *The Holiness–Pentecostal Movement in the United States* (Grand Rapids, Mich.: W. B. Eerdmans, 1971).

religious practice designed to "seek" the second blessing associated with being filled with the Holy Ghost.[21] It should be emphasized that in keeping with the spirit of "evangelism" the theological principles were not simply dry ideas but had very visible manifestations and strong personal effects. Thus, theological disputes that arose did not deal solely with esoteric abstractions but were connected to "lived experience." The fights and fissures that later developed within the churches, then, were not simply a matter of the efficacy of abstractions but were concerned with their ontology and, therefore, necessity.

The Pentecostal churches as discrete organizational entities grew out of an older revival movement that developed within the established mainline churches under the rubric of the National Holiness Association. This group was interdenominational in leadership and participation but was predominantly Methodist.[22] This movement and the organization it gave rise to grew up after the Civil War as an effort to combat the religious inertia and moral decay of the times. Inaugurated at a Vineland, New Jersey, camp meeting in 1867, the movement was preceded by a short-lived religious revival that swept the South in the wake of the Civil War defeat:

In the dark days following the war, the impoverished states of the defeated Confederacy turned to religion for solace. During 1865–67, "a sound of revival" was heard from one border to the other. The journals of Methodism teemed with news of great evangelistic efforts. The bishops of the Methodist Episcopal Church, South, meeting in General Conference in 1866, called for a return to Wesleyan principles as an answer to the post-war moral crisis. . . . In 1870, the bishops of the Southern church again called for a re-emphasis on sanctification: "Nothing is so much needed at the present time throughout all these lands as a general and powerful revival of scriptural holiness." [23]

The Vineland camp meeting was the result of a call issued by a group of clergymen to all, "irrespective of denominationalities

21. Vinson Synan, *Holiness–Pentecostal Movement,* p. 20.
22. Ibid., p. 45.
23. Ibid., pp. 34–35.

... who feel themselves comparatively isolated in their profession of holiness." [24] Such persons were requested to come "and make common supplication for the descent of the Spirit upon ourselves, the church, the nation, and the world." The meeting signified the beginning of a movement that greatly influenced the churches nationally until the turn of the century and dominated the life of the Baptist and Methodist churches in the South.[25] As noted earlier, the movement was regarded as a vehicle to counter the religious inertia of the times. It theologically sought to restore Wesley's doctrine of "entire sanctification" (that is, the "double cure"), to renew among the masses a desire for a life of holiness on a day-to-day level. It sought to restore "heart religion" and its traditional religious practices— plain dress, "spirited congregational singing," the mourners' bench, the camp meeting, shouting, and so on (in short, "that old-time religion")—which had been abandoned during the war and did not revive afterward as the mainline churches, especially the Methodist church in the North, became churches of the middle classes.[26] It was partially successful in this effort, as regards both belief and practice, throughout the country and especially in the South. "The predisposition to conceive of Christianity in terms of an orthodox belief-structure, which was later to be termed fundamentalism, and a particular means–end syndrome, namely revivalism, became almost ubiquitous among the Southern populace, fastening its grip even upon many of the descendants of Calvin and Knox." [27] During the height of the movement in Georgia Methodism, "200 of the 240 ministers of the North Georgia Conference professed to have received the experience of sanctification as a 'second blessing.' " [28]

Unfortunately, despite its huge success religiously in the South, the Holiness movement had little impact on the churches on the

24. Ibid., p. 36.
25. Hill, *Southern Churches*, pp. 13, 22–24.
26. Nichol, *Pentecostalism*, pp. 25–26.
27. Hill, *Southern Churches*, pp. 15–16.
28. Nichol, *Pentecostalism*, p. 39.

question of race, for it was precisely during this postwar period that Blacks were leaving and/or being forced out of southern churches and setting up their own ecclesiastical structures on a broad basis.[29] "In 1870, the Colored Methodist Episcopal Church was founded as a schism from the Methodist Church South. Ten years later, the National Baptist Convention was organized. The Primitive and Free-Will Baptists, along with the Cumberland Presbyterians, also experienced similar divisions. This trend continued until it was estimated that by 1929, 90% of all Negro Christians belonged to churches restricted to their own race."[30] It must also be noted that it was during the height of the Jim Crow period (1880–1910) that most of the major Holiness church organizations were established. Further, although various authors are at pains to soften the point, segregation of the races was/is a fact among those churches calling themselves Holiness and/or Pentecostal.[31]

Two of the Holiness churches founded during this period were Negro Holiness churches that would later become Pentecostal. One was the Church of God in Christ (popularly known as COGIC), which was incorporated in Memphis in 1897. This "group became the largest Negro Pentecostal sect in the world and the second largest of all the Pentecostal denominations in the United States."[32] The other Negro church was

the "United Holy Church," which began in 1886 near Wilmington, North Carolina in the town of Method. Other small bodies joined this church until 1902, when the formal organization of the denomination was effected with the help of W. H. Fulford, a Negro elder of the Fire-Baptized Holiness Church. This church generally followed the lead of the white Holiness churches of North Carolina, adopting after 1906 a statement of faith which placed the group in the Pentecostal family.... Although identical in doctrine with the Pentecostal

29. Although, in terms of the development of religious forms, their common attendance at services was important (see above, note 5).
30. Synan, *Holiness–Pentecostal Movement,* p. 166.
31. Ibid., p. 165.
32. Ibid., p. 80.

Holiness Church and the Church of God, the United Holy Church developed separately with a minimum of contact with its white sister denominations.[33]

It was from this church that Bishop Bromfield Johnson withdrew and established the Mount Calvary Holy Church in 1927.

A distinction must be made between the Holiness and Pentecostal movements because they became different organizational entities with, to some extent, different theological positions.[34] The differences that led to fissures among various Holiness groups, however, had personal roots in many cases—dissatisfaction over distribution of power and influence, use of funds, and so on.[35] The theological differences often recapitulate theological disputes that troubled the early Christian communities and had been settled by church councils early in the history of the church.

One such dispute, which in this case led to the creation of a new Pentecostal group, centered about the doctrine of the Holy Trinity. It began as a rejection of the conventional Trinitarian baptismal formula and asserted that "true baptism must be only 'in the name of Jesus' rather than 'in the name of the Father, of the Son, and of the Holy Ghost' " and escalated to a denial of the ontological status of the Trinity, asserting that there was only one Person in God, Jesus.[36] This new teaching spread rapidly

33. Ibid., p. 167.
34. The conventional distinction between Pentecostal and other churches is that, according to Pentecostals, one must receive the baptism of the Spirit, manifested by "speaking in tongues" (Acts 2:4). The Pentecostals developed out of Holiness churches which, as noted before, argued that one must receive the double cure. This was in contradistinction to the mainline churches, which preached a single baptism. Thus the Pentecostal and Holiness churches share a basic agreement about the necessity of a second experience. This in turn separates them from the mainline churches. Pentecostal and Holiness churches differ on the character of this second experience. Pentecostalists argue that "unless you get it like in Acts 2:4, you ain't got it," whereas the Holiness people are more variable.
35. Nichol (*Pentecostalism*, pp. 137–38) discusses the expulsion in 1923 of A. J. Tomlinson, General Overseer of The Church of God, over questions of money and abuse of authority.
36. Ibid., p. 90.

among Pentecostals, especially the Assemblies of God, and resulted in a new church body, the Pentecostal Assemblies of the
World. Another basis for dispute was the doctrine of "entire
sanctification," that is, whether there was need for a "second
work of grace" wherein the believer would be filled with the
Spirit or whether this "second work" was superfluous because
salvation, which is an inward work, changes both a man's heart
and his nature. Thus, the "old man" is "crucified," that is, "dead
with Christ." Other doctrinal issues involved divorce and remar-
riage, the mode of baptism, and the use of wine or grape juice
in Communion. Difficulties also arose over secular practice, for
example, whether one could eat pork, participate in the military
or labor unions, use coffee or tea, attend parties, and so on.[37]
All these were sources of conflict and often division among these
churches. In the case of the Mount Calvary Holy Church, the
division was not doctrinal but personal and political. The major
difference between the religious practice of Mount Calvary members and those in the United Holy Church is that the former
maintain a separation between the song and testimony services
whereas most other churches, including the United Holy Church,
allow members to preface their testimony with a hymn.[38]

The Pentecostal Movement

The doctrinal precedent for the distinction between
Holiness and Pentecostal churches was provided by B. H. Irwin
who in the 1880s preached throughout the South that the recep-

---

37. Liston Pope, *Millhands and Preachers* (New Haven: Yale University Press, 1942), p. 202, shows that the churches were, for the most
part, against the Gastonia textile workers' strike. The same stance was
taken by the Pentecostals. "Organizers in the T.W.O.C. complained frequently that 'revivalists' branded them as 'agents of the devil, with the
mark of the beast on our foreheads,' and destroyed embryonic unions at
a number of places." He also notes, however, that some Pentecostal
ministers resident in the area and workers themselves supported the
strike publicly. See also Cayton and Drake, *Black Metropolis,* p. 649.
38. Personal communication with Mary Goodwin, church historian.

tion of the Holy Ghost and fire was subsequent to sanctification. Irwin did not preach that speaking in tongues was the sign of having received the Holy Ghost, but "this phenomenon was quite common among those who received 'the fire.' " [39] Although Irwin's teaching gained wide currency and his church grew quickly, most Holiness churches rejected this theological wrinkle. He did, however, set the precedent and helped to produce the theological climate out of which the Pentecostal movement proper arose.

The official genesis of the Pentecostal movement is usually traced to one of two sources and persons—either the Azusa Street revival in Los Angeles in 1906 in which W. J. Seymour was the central figure or the Bible school run by Charles Parham in Topeka, Kansas, from 1900 to 1901. Parham had begun his career as a Methodist pastor, and during this period he both received and taught the experience of entire sanctification as a second work of grace. He adopted the idea of faith healing from contact with the more radical elements of the Holiness movement and also accepted the "third experience" teaching of Irwin's Fire-Baptized Church, although he rejected its extreme emotionalism. In 1894, the Methodist church, South, at its general conference had rejected the basic theological premise of the Holiness movement, namely, the idea of sanctification as a second work of grace. In the wake of the bitter struggle between Holiness and non-Holiness Methodists that led to that rejection, most of the Holiness denominations were formed, and many of these later became Pentecostal.[40] Parham himself left the Methodist church during this period, opening a "divine healing home" in Topeka, Kansas, in 1898 and a Bible school in 1900. It was here that the principle that defines the present Pentecostals was refined. Sanctification was not to be confused with the baptism of the Holy Spirit. "It was rather a 'third experience' separate in time and nature from the 'second blessing.' Sanctification cleansed and purified the believer, while the Baptism with the Holy Spirit

39. Nichol, *Pentecostalism*, p. 65.
40. Synan, *Holiness–Pentecostal Movement*, pp. 50–54.

brought great power for service. The only Biblical evidence that one had received the 'baptism' was the act of speaking with other tongues, as the other 120 disciples had done on the day of Pentecost. . . . One should not be satisfied, therefore, until he had spoken with tongues as "proof" that he had received the Holy Ghost." [41]

Parham's school and teaching achieved widespread popularity, but it was due to the famous Azusa Street revival that his teachings swept the South. W. J. Seymour, the central figure in the revival, was originally a Baptist preacher who later pastored a small Holiness church near Houston. When Parham reopened his Bible school in Houston, Seymour became one of his students. From there, he went to Los Angeles to assume the pastorate of a small group of Negroes who had been expelled from their Baptist church because of their Holiness views. They rejected, his Parham-derived doctrine, however, and he moved first into a private home where he continued evangelizing and later into an abandoned Methodist church on Azusa Street. The practices reported at the revival he opened there did not seem too different from those of the conventional Holiness revival, though speaking in tongues was explicitly associated with the baptism of the Spirit as a doctrinal principle. "Men and women would shout, weep, dance, fall into trances, speak and sing in tongues and interpret the messages in English." [42] The revival continued at Azusa Street for three years, and news of it rapidly spread throughout the city and around the country. In the South, many became familiar with the revival through the regular reports of F. Bartleman in the *Way of Faith* newspaper, but "the conversion of most of the Holiness movement in the Southeast to the Pentecōstal view" [43] was due to the efforts of G. B. Cashwell, a member of the Pentecostal Holiness Church, and C. H. Mason, the founder of the Church of God in Christ, who returned from Los Angeles to evangelize and proselytize in Dunn, North Carolina, in January 1907. As a result of the Dunn revival, the

41. Ibid., pp. 103–4.
42. Ibid., p. 108.
43. Ibid., p. 124.

United Holy Church adopted a "statement of faith which placed the group in the Pentecostal family." [44] Thus, the Mount Calvary Holy Church, an offshoot of the United Holy Church, may also be considered within the Pentecostal field, although the litmus test of the vernacular does not apply: "Unless you get it like in Acts 2:4, you ain't been saved."

The theological ferment that led the Pentecostal movement to separate from the Holiness movement continued through the first two decades of the twentieth century. The "Jesus only" controversy was one source of conflict. Another was the "finished work" doctrine of W. H. Durham, who had also gone to Azusa Street and returned a convert to the new Pentecostal doctrine. He was the pastor of a mission in Chicago and was originally a Baptist, although he preached the Wesleyan view of sanctification. In 1910, however, he arrived at a new theological position. "Calling his new doctrine the 'Finished Work,' Durham called for a new view which assigned sanctification to the act of conversion based on the 'finished work of Christ on Calvary.' Denying Wesley's concept of 'residue of sin' in the believer, he taught that one was perfectly sanctified at conversion and had no need of a 'second change' later." [45] It should be noted that this doctrine is similar to, although it goes much beyond, the position taken by the Methodist church, South, in 1894, when it wrested control of the church from the Holiness wing. The Methodist statement disputed the monopoly on truth claimed by the Holiness people. Durham's teaching, on the other hand, attacked the doctrinal basis of the Pentecostal movement and denied its claim to any truth. Needless to say, the conflict that ensued was of major proportions. In the end, the southern churches remained Trinitarian, and the "finished work" doctrine became most popular among urban independent churches.

By 1920, much of the theological ferment had subsided, and most of the organizational lines of the movement were set, al-

---

44. Ibid., p. 167. Mount Calvary people (at least in Boston) do not, however, preach the necessity of glossolalia as a sign of the Spirit.
45. Ibid., p. 149.

Z89.9   P218b
C.1

though fissures have continued on a smaller scale. The southern churches maintained their original doctrinal positions, remaining solidly Trinitarian and Wesleyan regarding sanctification. It can also be said that their various doctrinal differences are outweighed by their basic similarities in dogma and practice. The southern churches generally (including the non-Holiness denominations) stress an evangelical Christianity and maintain a tendency toward perfectionism that is unique to the region.[46] The major differences involved practice, for although (until quite recently) most of southern Protestantism preached a similar evangelical line, maintaining a biblical fundamentalism and an old-line moral stand, the middle- and upper-class members deviated from this position, especially in practice, whereas the Pentecostals maintained a much closer link between theory and practice. It should be noted also that the Holiness–Pentecostal movement had begun as a broad-based religious movement, but by the 1920s Pentecostalism was restricted to the lower classes. This was especially true in the case of Blacks and accounts for part of the large differences between the rural in-migrants and the indigenous Blacks of the northern cities.[47] Regional differences— northern Protestantism's accommodation to the "modern world" and continued condemnation of "conformity to the world" in the South—account for yet more. Why these migrating Blacks were not at home in northern Black churches is obvious, yet their alienation was much deeper than simply a feeling of being out of

46. "In sum, the prevalent diversities within southern Protestantism are minimized by the striking sameness within and between denominations. The radical wings of all four dominated their respective modes of life in the South. The elements of the four heritages, which maximized the Bible, informal congregational association, personal holiness, and inward religion—in other words, the most evangelical parties of the four families—early gained the upper hand. An approximate regional consensus was actualized, and in the case of the Baptist and Methodist denominations, a remarkable unanimity of purpose and method resulted." Hill, *Southern Churches,* p. 76. See also W. W. Wood, *Culture and Personality Aspects of the Pente-Holiness Religion* (Paris: Mouton, 1965), p. 9.
47. Cayton and Drake, *Black Metropolis,* pp. 613, 636 ff.

place in the "cold formality" of northern "high-toned" churches. The southern churches were evangelical and defined the world in religious terms. Though both stances were dead letters in northern Protestantism, these epistemological and theological issues went far beyond the level of emotionalism in the church service.[48] It was thus inevitable that southern Blacks would resurrect their former religious traditions in urban settings. At the same time the generally impoverished circumstances of these migrants severely limited their options and opportunities in the church marketplace—thus the rise of small, lower-class Black congregations, popularly known as storefronts.

There were, of course, great differences between these new congregations and the established northern churches. The new churches maintained the demonstrative worship style and fundamentalist literalism of the milieu from which they came. The established churches had been making progressive accommodation to the new urban and industrial world that emerged in the North in the latter part of the nineteenth century. They had become in fact "sober middle-class churches," increasingly "secularized" in outlook.[49] Such churches had no appeal for the southern migrants who, though no longer peasants, were still products of an evangelical tradition and a religious world view. These new urban dwellers were forced to reconstitute their religious traditions under the harsh socioeconomic conditions of the Depression. Without funds for new edifices, they had to take what they could get in the way of facilities, acquiring buildings from fleeing Whites, or converting commercial space. Only those denominations with well-developed bureaucracies and resources could acquire land and edifices easily. These better-off churches were usually already established in the cities and served a middle-

48. Most of these doctrinal distinctions, however, are firmer in theory than in practice and are of increasingly less import. Thus, in terms of our effort, it is not especially useful to distinguish between Holiness and Pentecostal churches, and that distinction will be reserved for special cases. The generic "Pentecostal–Holiness churches" will otherwise suffice.
49. Cayton and Drake, *Black Metropolis*, pp. 634–36.

and/or upper-class congregation, for example, Methodists, Presbyterians, Episcopalians. (The Catholic church chose to concentrate on saving the faith of the Irish and Italian immigrants and therefore neglected the southern migrants for the most part.)

The rise of lower-class urban congregations within storefronts was the product of a historical process rooted in the rise of Holiness and Pentecostal churches as manifestations of reforming zeal within American and especially southern Protestantism. The subsequent exhaustion of this impulse among the middle and upper classes led to the confining of this tendency to the lower classes, Black and White, where it continued to flourish. Blacks who moved north and west as part of the Great Migrations became carriers of this perfectionist impulse, along with their other religious traditions. As a large and impoverished population confined mainly to ghettos, these Black migrants placed enormous pressures upon available institutional resources; and their choices in the market for church edifices were and continue to be severely limited. These pressures, coupled with their history, led to the storefront phenomenon among urban Black (and Latin) populations.

Given this background and history, it is plain that the conventional view of storefront churches as exotic, esoteric religious expressions inferior to the mainline denominations is simply erroneous. Also erroneous is the tendency to label all the groups that occupied storefronts "sects and cults." [50] Christian churches of several different denominations occupied storefronts, and although they shared a basic southern Christianity, there were theological and practical differences among them. These bodies in turn should not be confused with the welter of other spiritualist, nationalist, or neo-African groups that also used commercial

50. See James E. Blackwell, "A Comparative Study of Five Negro Storefront Churches in Cleveland" (master's thesis, Case Western Reserve University, 1949). See also Arthur H. Fauset, *Black Gods of the Metropolis* (Philadelphia: University of Pennsylvania Press, 1944); cf. Thomas R. Frazier, "An Analysis of Social-Scientific Writing on American Negro Religion" (Ph.D. diss., Columbia University, 1967), chap. 5.

space.[51] The point is that storefront churches do not constitute a substantive category. Storefronts are a physical characteristic that many groups share. Insofar as the churches were concerned, as soon as they were able to build or buy a standard church edifice, they did so. Many large Baptist churches of today had humble beginnings in a storefront. Far from being an aberration, the storefront phenomenon was (a) the locus of resurrection by Blacks from the South of their distinctive religious traditions, and (b) the vehicle they were forced to use due to their poverty amid the conditions of the Depression. It was the physical environment wherein many Black Pentecostal–Holiness churches were established.

As for Pentecostal churches in particular, their congregations tend to be quite small—in most cases less than fifty members—and, like other churches, are predominantly females.[52] Although these small churches probably outnumber the larger, more respectable ones, and although they are closer to the rural traditions of the masses than the "better" churches, they are given

51. "[F]raternal solidarity and unity within a self-assertive, separate, and more powerful black existence was the answer to the black man's problems. This conviction was kept alive in the black ghettos early in this century by rebel–prophets whose mission, expressed with pentecostal vigor, sought to transform the malaise of recurrent failure and despair into the instruments of final, apocalyptic salvation. Marcus Garvey, Noble Drew Ali, W. D. Fard, Elijah Muhammad, and countless itinerant street-messiahs were of this vein, sent, they said, from heaven itself to curb white racism and rescue their people from the bottomless pit of society. They were gods of the metropolis calling the faithful and the faithless back to the fold, and their message of 'black folks working for black folks' came from the depths of the black urban experience." Thomas L. Blair, *Retreat to the Ghetto* (New York: Hill and Wang, 1977), pp. 28–29.

52. Cayton and Drake (*Black Metropolis*) note fewer than thirty-five members in their studies; Blackwell in "Five Storefront Churches" notes fifty-one, but his figures are skewed by one very large church. A number of people claim that there are many more men in the Church of God in Christ, equal to or even greater than the number of women.

short shrift in the literature.[53] The number of these churches mushroomed in the thirties and forties and paralleled the northern migrations of the Black population. As noted, this was dismissed as the "storefront phenomenon" and treated as ephemeral and peripheral to the religious mainstream. This view has only recently been challenged.[54] Such an attitude missed two important points: these churches provided the recently arrived southerners, especially those of peasant origins, with a nexus of social connections and a web of relationships as well as an ideological framework for dealing with a new world; the Pentecostal churches in particular, as heirs to the post–Civil War Holiness movement within American Protestantism, represent the religious revival of a Christianity that had become "conformed to the world." Despite the available evidence, neither the storefront phenomenon nor Pentecostalism was placed in any meaningful historical context. Rather than being seen as "normal," these churches are pictured in the literature as marginal, esoteric institutions of questionable stability and with psychologically maladjusted memberships, drawn from the most destitute elements of the population and further exploited by the machinations of unscrupulous preachers.[55] Though it is true that these churches were confined to the lower classes and that there were and continue to be abuses by "jackleg" preachers, the case is overdrawn and neglects the Depression context in which this storefront phenomenon developed. In a less desperate social context, there would have been other "hustles" available to those so inclined. In the present case, there is little evidence of the "Let Us Prey"

53. It is also true that access to these churches has been limited apparently. Fauset (*Black Gods*) and Blackwell ("Five Storefront Churches"), both indicated some difficulty. This may be one reason for the limited studies.

54. J. R. Washington, *Black Sects and Cults* (New York: Anchor Doubleday, 1973).

55. See Fauset, *Black Gods,* and Blackwell, "Five Storefront Churches," for examples of this approach. See also Frazier, "Analysis," p. 151.

attitude, although there are examples of ministers who are accused of living well at the expense of their flocks.[56]

In summary, then, the Pentecostal movement with which we are specifically concerned should be seen as part of a wider religious revival within American Protestantism that followed the Civil War. This larger revival movement was in turn but another in a succession of reform movements that arise within Christianity as a whole whenever belief and practice decline. Pentecostalism arose among Blacks initially as a southern extension of the Holiness movement. Its rise as an urban phenomenon (storefront churches) parallels the northern and urban migrations of southern and initially rural Blacks. This focus on these churches as a religious revival and as part of a larger resurrection among the lower classes of their particular religious traditions provides a ready rubric for separating the churches from the non-Christian religious and cultural groups.[57] Earlier writers, who attached secondary importance to ideologies and their influence on behavior, were led by the structural similarities of the various groups to view them all in the same light; but structural similarities are insufficient reason to group them in one category. The goals and beliefs of these groups are of equal importance in categorization. Moreover, they determine for the group itself the character and meaning of its action, and this action and its meaning (praxis) are the locus of concern here. The effort is thus to view a particular Pentecostal church, the Mount Calvary Holy Church, in light of the nature and meaning of its action and the position of the church and its members within the larger context of Black life in Boston.

56. Ira de A. Reid, "Let Us Prey," *Opportunity* 4 (September 1926): 274–78.
57. For example, Daddy Grace, Father Divine, Black Jews, Spiritualists, and so on.

T W O
Mount Calvary History

The history and development of the Mount Calvary Holy Church of America, Inc., are rooted in the rise of the Holiness and Pentecostal movements in the post–Civil War era and more specifically in the fission within these movements that produced separate Black ecclesiastical organizations in the closing years of the last century. A sketch of this broader development was presented in chapter 1; in this chapter the specific development of Mount Calvary church will be outlined. It is not my intention to produce a full-fledged history of the church. The goal here is to follow the thread of Pentecostal–Holiness development in specific regard to this particular church, thereby showing the continuities one with the other and providing some necessary background details for the ensuing analysis of the Mount Calvary Boston churches.

Because this area of Black church development is virtually untouched by scholars, a documentary base for comparison of Mount Calvary with similar churches hardly exists. It should be noted, however, that the Mount Calvary case appears to parallel the experience of other Black churches—a series of relatively small congregations organized by a strong, beloved, and charismatic leader, occasional schisms, and so on—and thus is representative of a broader range of experience. Bishop Mason, for example, founder of the Church of God in Christ (COGIC), presided over the large-scale growth of his church and died in 1961 when he was in his nineties. COGIC is the largest of the

Black Pentecostal–Holiness churches and has experienced large-scale numerical growth. Its growth has far exceeded Mount Calvary's, although this may be partially attributed to an earlier and more spectacular start. In 1926, for example, this church already comprised 733 congregations with a total membership of 30,263; in 1970 the organization had grown to some 8,000 congregations with a total of 1 million members. It has been experiencing the same transformation of its membership's socioeconomic status as is evident in the Mount Calvary churches in Boston, although the transformation within COGIC is reputed to be on a much larger scale than that in the Mount Calvary church. The essential point to be made here, however, is that the development of the Mount Calvary Holy Church, especially in its more recent growth, is by no means unique; rather, it shares a number of characteristics with other churches from the same tradition.[1]

As noted earlier, the Mount Calvary Holy Church is a splinter group of the United Holy Church. Its founder was the late Bishop Bromfield Johnson. In the mid-1920s, he broke away from the United Holy Church after a dispute with the leaders of that church and founded Mount Calvary.[2] The church was chartered in Boston in 1929. For the rest of his life, Bishop Johnson traveled extensively, preaching and founding churches. At his death in 1972, there were "eighty churches in thirteen states." [3]

1. Walter J. Hollenweger, "Black Pentecostal Concept," *Concept,* Special Issue, no. 30 (June 1970).
2. "He decided to withdraw from the body and continue his work independent of them. This he did at a conference held in Summit, New York in 1929. ... After one or two preliminary meetings, they met in Conference in Boston, Massachusetts and adopted substantially the principles now held. At this meeting, they decided to call themselves 'The Mt. Calvary Holy Church of America, Inc.' " *Manual* of the Mount Calvary Holy Church, p. 3.
3. At this and other points, the study suffers from lack of reliable documentation—a common problem when studying religious groups and organizations. See B. Y. Landis, "Confessions of a Church Statistician," in Schneider, *Religion, Culture, and Society.* Written records were difficult to obtain. This figure is the popularly agreed upon one for the size of the church.

Bishop Johnson grew up in a large family in Charlotte and Henderson, North Carolina. His parents were Baptists, and his father was a church deacon. "His mother was religious and very strict also." [4] Both his parents worked; his father was employed in the railroad yards, and his mother ran a restaurant in Charlotte.[5] His father died when Johnson was nine, and his mother gave up the restaurant because it was too much to carry alone and did "day's work," that is, domestic work, instead. After the father's death, the family lived in Durham, North Carolina, for a while and then moved to Henderson to live with an aunt. While in Durham, Bishop Johnson became affiliated with the United Holy Church. His widow recalls Bishop Johnson in his youth:

You know they would have these revivals and his mother would get happy and "Hon" (Bishop Johnson), he would sing, you know. Then they had a meeting over at the United Holy Church, you know that was Bishop Fisher, and they would all go over there. His mother used to go every night and she would get happy. He would stay outside, you know, at first. Then it seemed something began to draw him into this church, and come to find out he and his mother both were on the floor shouting together. Then he got convicted or something and he and his mother both joined this church. He took an active part in the church. They asked him to lead devotions and he could really beat a tambourine. They used to bring tambourines to church just so Bromfield could beat it. So that's when he got connected up with the United Holy Church.

Later, when the family moved to Henderson, "they had a United Holy Church there in Henderson where he attended." [6] He was nearly sixteen at this time. He was religious at an early age, and his talents were put to use early; there are several stories of his ministry as a "boy wonder." It is clear, moreover, that he was

4. Interview with Mother Louise Johnson, widow of the founder.
5. The southern Blacks of this period were still pretty much a rural peasantry. Bishop Johnson's father had an industrial job, and the family operated a business. Given the time, Bishop Johnson's family was clearly of higher socioeconomic status than the mass of southern Blacks of this period.
6. Interview with Mother Louise Johnson.

preaching and conducting revivals while in his late teens. He married in December 1919 and moved his bride to Henderson where he continued his evangelistic work.[7] In 1923–24, he assumed a pastorate in East Orange, New Jersey, later moving to Summit, New York, to pastor a United Holy Church there. While still serving as pastor in New York, he went to Boston to preach a revival at the invitation of a Reverend Mr. Chandler from Cambridge. Out of that revival, he started a United Holy Church in Boston.

Both his popularity as an evangelist and his following within the church increased, which caused trouble for him with the elders of the church, who attempted to curtail his influence. As a result of this conflict, he left the United Holy Church and founded the Mount Calvary Holy Church of America, Inc. The rituals and practices adopted by the new church were almost identical with those of the United Holy Church.[8] Approximately 200 people followed him from the United Holy Church into this new body.[9] A church was begun in Boston and, shortly afterward, another in East Orange. Unfortunately, neither church lasted long, "because he wasn't able to stay there." It was from these beginnings, however, that the present group of Mount Calvary churches arose.

Bishop Johnson was primarily an evangelist and continued this style of ministry throughout the Depression years and until his death. These evangelistic journeys were the basic mechanism in the growth of the Mount Calvary churches. Johnson would receive an invitation to preach a revival, and if the revival were successful, resulting in the "saving of many souls," he would start a church from that group. He would remain with the new church for a short period and then move on, leaving a minister in

7. According to his widow, she met him in 1918 or early 1919, at which time he would have been seventeen or eighteen. She said he was already preaching and running revivals.

8. Interview with Mary Goodwin, who was writing the official history of the church.

9. *Manual* of the Mount Calvary Holy Church, p. 3. There is some evidence that this figure may be inflated.

charge and returning periodically to check on progress.[10] Thus, he was constantly on the road, visiting established churches, starting new ones, and preaching revivals.

He traveled with groups called "evangelistic teams." Three of these teams traveled with him during the course of his life. They were made up of young people, male and female, who were attracted to him and helped in his ministry. The numbers varied, but there were usually five persons to a team. The team's function was twofold: (*a*) to make up the initial congregation for the meetings and revivals, and (*b*) to assist in the preparation and running of the services—cleaning up beforehand and afterward, playing the organ and piano, and leading the devotions during the services.[11] Because of the intimacy of association and the strong bonds that consequently developed, former team members retained their loyalty to the founder and remained affiliated with the church. Team members tended to marry each other, and when they began courting they were "retired." Such marriages helped bind them still closer to the church. Many pastors and other officers of the church were former evangelistic team members.[12] These teams were active until the mid-1960s when they ceased to function because the members of the last group became

10. Interview with the Reverend Christy Belle Livingston.

11. "Because when he would go around to try and open a church, he had to have his own congregation because they wouldn't help him. He had a piano player, one could sing, and the other could read the Scripture; so he had his own congregation. And by the girls being young, people would come out to see the young girls in religious work." Interview with Mother Louise Johnson.

12. A source of contention has been that members of the founder's church family replaced his real family in terms of influence in the councils of the church. Real power was held by those who were associated with him, especially those who were members of the evangelistic teams. An important point here is the prominence of women in the church organization. Mother L. Johnson noted that women in the church had started, bought, and built churches and were recognized by "Dad" (Bishop Johnson) as the equal of men in the church. Of the nine officials holding national staff positions at the 1972 Convocation, four were women.

involved with the care of individual congregations. Bishop Johnson continued to travel until his death in 1972.

The evangelistic teams traveled by car. Though detailed information as to how this work was financed is unavailable, it is apparent that it was not a money-making operation. The teams lived on "the mercy of the Lord," and there was rarely any money to send home for the support of Bishop Johnson's family.[13] Moreover, Bishop Johnson often contributed his own money to help various churches in financial difficulties.

At present there are churches scattered throughout cities in the Southeast, Northeast, and Midwest. As noted earlier, the figure publicly agreed upon is "eighty churches in thirteen states." (This seems somewhat exaggerated, but there is no way to check the figures independently.) The growth of the church nationally seems to have greatly slowed or stabilized. There is a "revolving-door" phenomenon whereby new members simply take the places of others who leave. The size of the church remains roughly the same, although new members are constantly being added. This is also true of entire congregations. At the death of the founder, several churches in Connecticut, "pulled out" and went independent, forming their own body. Their loss was offset when one or two formerly independent churches joined the Mount Calvary body. During the last year of fieldwork for this study (1973), some Washington, D.C., churches severed their ties and became independent; other churches continue, however, to replace those that leave.[14]

13. Interviews with Mother Louise Johnson and Nathaniel Johnson.
14. In 1972, soon after the founder's death, the Reverend A. Tucker and the churches she pastored in Connecticut pulled out. At the National Convocation that year, a Reverend Mr. Owens from Washington, D.C., brought his church into the organization. In 1973, the Reverend Early Edwards from Washington, D.C., went independent with the churches he pastored. At the same time, however, a Reverend Mr. Brandon of Virginia and a Sister Geary of Raleigh, North Carolina, brought their churches into the body. There are usually personal and financial reasons involved when a church leaves the body. By going independent, the individual minister may gain more recognition and authority and be relieved of the financial burden of support of the national body. Con-

The present Boston churches were started in the early 1960s
and were among the last begun by the founder. There had been
Mount Calvary churches in Boston on two earlier occasions: the
original church established in 1929 and a mission under Elder
Lewis in the 1940s.[15] Both these ventures folded. There remained, however, the need and desire for a church in Boston, especially as the church had been chartered in Massachusetts.

In 1959 Bishop Johnson came to Boston and acquired a house
on Townsend Street and, later, a church in the South End. The
latter building had belonged to Bishop Young and the Church of
God in Christ (COGIC). Prior to its use by his congregation, it
had been a livery stable and a feed house.[16] Bishop Johnson and
members of his evangelistic team refurbished and lived in the
house on Townsend Street. After some months in Boston, the
bishop returned to his evangelistic travels and made one of his
sons pastor of this church (hereafter referred to as Alpha). Another building was acquired during the winter of 1960 that became the headquarters of the national church (hereafter referred
to as Beta) after the previous headquarters in Buffalo, New
York, burned down. This building had been a large synagogue
and yeshiva in the Dorchester section of Boston. The third
church (hereafter referred to as Gamma) was organized in 1962
and is pastored by an elderly woman who had been a longtime
member of one of the United Holy churches in Boston. She had
left that church in the wake of some disagreement and subsequently opened a storefront under the Mount Calvary banner in
Mattapan. Hers was the smallest of the three Boston churches
and the most tenuous in terms of its organization.

The Alpha church is located on Shawmut Avenue in the South

---

versely, some independent churches desire a closer fellowship and affiliation with a vital organization and are willing, literally, to pay the price
for these benefits.

15. Interview with the Reverend Christy Belle Livingston.

16. Interview with Elder Granville. The casual observer would assume
it to be a storefront. The use of this term was rejected, interestingly, not
because of its pejorative connotation but because of the edifice's prior
use as a church by Bishop Young's congregation.

End in a decaying part of the city. It is opposite a new low-income housing project and a recently completed moderate- and middle-income development. As part of the Model Cities urban renewal area, the neighborhood has lost much of its older housing stock and other structures, and the church itself is in danger of being taken for urban renewal purposes.[17] The new housing developments have replaced some of the older buildings, but a great deal of vacant land remains near the church. The neighborhood is primarily a low-income one (the new moderate- and middle-income project is a major exception), predominantly Black and Latin in ethnic composition, and with poor commercial facilities. Shawmut Avenue is noteworthy for its large number of churches. At the time of this study, there were four other churches within a block of the Alpha church—a United House of Prayer, a Church of God, a Baptist church, and a Hispanic Pentecostal church. The number has recently been reduced, the Baptist church having sold its large building to a neighboring Pentecostal organization and moved to a still larger structure on Tremont Street.[18] The new owners renovated the structure and vacated their old building, which is currently empty. At the moment, there are four active churches on that block, with several more to the north, also on Shawmut Avenue.

The Beta church is on a small residential street off Blue Hill Avenue in the Dorchester section of Boston near Grove Hall. Blue Hill Avenue used to be a large shopping area for the Jewish community that formerly lived in the Roxbury and lower Dorchester sections. Since the late fifties, the familiar process of neighborhood succession has been in progress, and the area is now predominantly Black. The church's property was acquired during the Jewish exodus and was purchased from Whites. The Blue Hill Avenue shopping district was heavily damaged during

17. Subsequent to the completion of the fieldwork, the church was appropriated by the urban renewal authorities (fall 1973). The congregation has since found new headquarters in Dorchester.
18. The building was initially offered to Alpha church. The pastor and deacon inspected it and decided it was not worth the $60,000 that was being asked.

the riots of the middle sixties and still bears the scars. The church, however, although only a half block from the thoroughfare, is in a different ambience altogether. It is surrounded by large, private homes that are fairly well kept, and the street has been unmarked by the kind of neighborhood decay that characterizes the South End location of Alpha church. The immediate population around Beta church is almost all Black. There are a number of churches in the vicinity, but the density of churches is not so great as in the Alpha church neighborhood.

The Gamma church is on Norfolk Street in Dorchester. This is a major thoroughfare in upper Dorchester and was still a "changing neighborhood" so that there are a number of Whites still in the area. The church is in a commercial building, a frame structure about thirty feet deep and fifty feet wide. The width is due to the apparent elimination of a central partition that divided the structure into two parts. It is quite small and comfortably holds no more than forty or fifty people. The Alpha church is somewhat larger, and the Beta church larger still. It has two wings, one of which is used regularly for church services and holds 200-300 people easily. The other wing is used for larger revivals, church meetings, and convocations and holds almost 1,000 people seated both on the ground floor and in an upstairs balcony.

In terms of membership, the Gamma church is most problematic. The elderly pastor is unable to be very active in the building of the church. She has difficulty walking, lives far from the church, does not have a car, and must depend on others for transportation. More importantly, her services are invariably late in starting, often by an hour or more. Busy adults with families and work obligations are simply unable to abide her scheduling. Her membership is thus quite small and includes a number of children whom she picks up or has picked up.[19] The Alpha church has also had a small membership, which has fluctuated in the

19. Simply put, she is no longer able to perform her pastoral role effectively. There is some recognition of this, and in unguarded moments people will say that "there are only two and a half Mount Calvary churches in Boston."

two decades of its existence. In 1963, when the founder's son gave up the pastorate, there were about twelve members. This number dwindled to one or two for a few years while the church was without a pastor and then increased to approximately thirty by 1970. Later, there was a sharp decline in members when a number of people left the church for various reasons; some moved away, and others had personal disagreements with other members or became alienated over particular issues. Currently there are about twelve members on the rolls, of whom seven or eight are quite active.[20]

The Beta church is different in several ways from the other two. It has a much larger physical plant and is thus much more expensive to maintain. To defray its greater costs, it needs and has acquired a much larger membership than the other two churches. Furthermore, as the national headquarters of the Mount Calvary Holy Church and the business center of the organization, it enjoyed the founder's presence more often than the other churches did. It was acquired in the winter of 1960 or the spring of 1961. The evangelistic team provided the initial congregation, and a deacon was "borrowed" from another church for official and legal reasons.[21] No members were admitted during the first year, and twelve people joined the following year when the church doors opened. The membership remained small for several years but has grown rapidly since then.[22] The present

20. Since 1973 the membership has been rising again. A number of members have been added who live near the church's new location on Talbot Avenue. Also, several members from Beta have transferred their membership to the Alpha church. Apparently the cycle of development is again on an upward path. See the Epilogue for a more extended discussion of these developments.

21. Mary Goodwin, the church historian, reported that "You'd hear all this noise, singing and clapping, and you'd go in and there'd only be just three people there."

22. More than one person claimed that two or three people are saved and join the Beta church each Sunday. This seems exaggerated, but it is true that, as a rule, people are saved at Sunday services at Beta and there are regular additions to the rolls. Mary Goodwin claimed that the membership has more than doubled in the last five years; the Reverend

adult membership runs between 110 and 120, with about the same number on the Sunday School rolls. The growth rate is higher at the Beta church than at the other two churches,[23] but there is a much greater turnover in membership—an instance of the revolving-door syndrome. There are a number of reasons for this high turnover—personal, political, and financial.[24] There is some public awareness of the situation, but it is not perceived by those in authority as a problem requiring remedy. There is, moreover, a fairly stable core of actively involved faithful (between thirty and fifty people), who attend most of the services and take part in most of the activities; they are fervent in religious practice and liberal in their giving. At times, though, it seemed that there were almost two churches: the "actives" and the "Sunday-only" others. This is, however, a common pattern for voluntary organizations generally and not just for Protestant churches that lack the strictures requiring constant attendance that are the rule in the Roman Catholic church.

The finances of the Boston churches are another indication of the scope of their operations. The church year begins and ends in August with the National Convocation. For the 1972 church year, the total of all money raised in Boston by the three congregations was $30,000. For the 1973 church year, the sum declined by about $1,000. The Beta church, which raises the bulk of the total, contributed $22,000 in 1972 and 1973; the Alpha church

Nathaniel Johnson asserted that it has increased by one third since he left in 1968.

23. Less than ten people have joined the Alpha church in the last two years.

24. I was unable to interview many persons who had left the church. Those current members who commented on this issue emphasized three main points: (*a*) the heavy financial obligation they felt as members of Beta church; (*b*) the centralization of authority in the pastor's hands; and (*c*) their inability to put their talents to satisfactory use. If one assumes that fifty people join the Beta church each year (one each Sunday), that is a 50 percent increase in membership, which should make a visible impact. Such is not the case. If there is such an increase, it has left no marks.

raised $6,800 in 1972 and $6,000 in 1973; the Gamma church raised less than $2,000 in both years.[25]

This is not a large amount of money; yet, given the small size of the churches, it is phenomenal (the total membership of the three congregations is much below 200). The Beta church, which cost nearly $70,000, paid off its indebtedness in ten years. The achievement is more readily apparent in the case of the Alpha church, where there were fewer than fifteen people on the rolls in 1972. Their total of $6,800 is one indication of the members' faith and support of their church.[26]

It should also be kept in mind that these three congregations are of recent vintage. As such, they may not be "typical" of the larger group of Mount Calvary churches nationally. Their development parallels the early stages of many Black congregations, however, and their growth parallels that of the Black ghetto as it moves southward in the Boston metropolitan area. The study of their development thus yields some perspective on the experience of these small Pentecostal and Holiness churches within the Boston context and sheds light on the processes by which churches such as these grow and operate within the metropolitan environment. Moreover, these three congregations do appear to be good examples of Black Pentecostal–Holiness churches in Boston.

In focusing on these three Mount Calvary Boston congregations, we have obviously not produced a full-fledged history of Mount Calvary in Boston. We have, however, elucidated the theological and organizational threads connecting Mount Calvary Holy Church, Inc., with a long-standing southern Holiness tradition. Further, the development of these Boston congregations

25. It was difficult to get information concerning church finances, a frustration frequently mentioned by interviewees. The author was discouraged in such efforts although never refused outright. At the 1972 National Convocation, there was a theft of financial records from the recording secretaries. Although never actually accused, the author was told by several members that he was one of those suspected.
26. Some say this reflects the ingenuity exercised in bringing pressure upon people to give.

exemplifies the way the founder built up his church, and these churches offer patterns of development similar to those of other Black Holiness and Pentecostal congregations in Boston. It is clear from our examination that the founder and those who worked with him in the establishment of the church were serious men and women of God, devoted to their task, and not exotic or aberrant. Nor were they interested in personal financial gain; for they would, in that case, have discovered a more remunerative line of work—obviously, the church did not "pay off" in those terms. It is also clear that the energies expended in missionary endeavor and their results were not epiphenomenal but arose out of genuine desires for the "furtherance of the Kingdom," the concomitant exigencies of ecclesiastical politics, and the real needs of the people for religious reform.

THREE
Ritual

Against the sociohistorical background within which the Boston Mount Calvary churches are situated, let us turn now to a close examination of the life of the church as seen through its rituals. It is readily apparent that the liturgical practice of the Mount Calvary Holy Church, Inc., is not unique. Rather, it shares basic features and patterns with other churches from the same historical tradition. Although all of these churches have their own distinctive touches, it would be fair to say that not only do their liturgies have features in common but they are, in fact, standardized. Given this fact, the ritual practices discussed herein are also relevant to discussions of the liturgical practices of churches arising more generally out of the Holiness–Pentecostal tradition. This standardization and the extended connections to other churches, however, are not the focus here; rather, we are concerned with these rituals as exemplifying the lifeblood of these Boston congregations. We shall deal with these rituals as composites (that is, as "typical" services, with no distinctions made among the various congregations, except where it was felt that to do so offered further clarity). The ensuing discussion is in three parts: (1) an overview, which describes the settings, frequency of observance, and types of services; (2) a synchronic discussion of a "typical" service; and (3) an analysis of the typical service as a sacred play, a ritual drama with a set of specified and structured roles, the purpose of which is not simply to provide a vehicle for worship but also to enable the believer to "approach (closely) the throne of grace" and even to encounter the Almighty directly.

The description of the service elements is deliberatedly detailed. My purpose is to place as much observational material in the text as possible and thereby to begin to correct a serious defect in the literature. There is relatively little direct observation available for analytical and comparative purposes, one factor that has contributed to the defective interpretations of Pentecostal practice. Providing a fund of descriptive material provides a standard for comparison with future work that did not exist for this effort and makes available to the reader part of the content of empirical observation on which my own interpretation is based.

Overview

The major business of the church is liturgical practice, the performance of religious ritual. This is the activity that occupies most of the time of church members as a group, in the sense that this is primarily what they *do* when they act together as a church. There are other things that are at least equally important in defining the church, but ritual performance is one of the most visible things that the church does, and it thus provides the defining characteristics of the church in the eyes of many outsiders. Insiders do not define the church in this way when queried on the subject, but for the vast majority of them this is the major part of the answer to the question, "What does one do as a church member?" Ritual and its practice must therefore be regarded as a crucial part of the church experience and considered with that in mind.

This activity is neither isolated nor meaningless. It is embedded in a framework of meaning and belief that informs and shapes it and makes it meaningful. Without this ontological and teleological frame, there would be little incentive to perform the activity. The ritual process is also the mechanism by which the ontological framework is made real in consciousness and history —thus the organizational implication of one pastor's comment:

"Salvation comes by hearing, and hearing by the Word of God. . . . I always believed that if the Lord saved you, He'd lead you to someone's church. Where else are you going to hear the Word?"

THE SETTINGS. The ritual life of the three congregations (and Mount Calvary Holy Church generally) is limited to the church edifices. Thus, the main function of the church building is as a place to "have church." There are occasions on which services are held in places other than the church building, but these are limited. Baptisms, for example, are sometimes conducted in country settings and not in baptismal pools (Mount Calvary practices full-immersion baptisms). The Beta church now has a large swimming pool that is used for this sacramental purpose, but the other two churches must use either the Beta pool, country lakes and ponds, or some other facility. Another example would be a congregation that has no building and conducts services in members' homes.[1] At present, the three Boston congregations have adequate facilities, although they all wish to improve their buildings.

The edifice is also important as a visible center of group life and as a meeting place, although this is less the case with the Beta church, which has considerable space outside the church for nonreligious activities. Status considerations are attached to the existing edifices, but these are confined to the clergy and everyone is more concerned with the quality of worship than with status; more accurately, the criteria for excellence lie in the vitality of worship rather than with the churches' physical elegance. Invidious comparison is often made between other churches and Mount Calvary on these criteria: "You know, we'll go to these churches and the building will be so beautiful, stained-glass windows, fine lines . . . and the service will be just

1. Gamma church met in the pastor's home before it secured a building on Norfolk Street. Such house churches are not unusual, even in Boston, and may be found wherever a group is unable to afford a regular edifice. Helen Phillips, in "Shouting for the Lord" (master's thesis, University of North Carolina, 1969), studied a prayer group that met at the leader's house in Chapel Hill.

as dry." Or again: "The Lord is not in some of these big churches
—it's dead in there—but go to some little church and the Spirit
will be just as high, the fellowship will be real. The Lord says,
'Where two or three are gathered together in My Name, I am
in the midst.' "

RITUAL PRACTICE. A substantial amount of time during the
week is devoted to ritual.[2] Members gather several times for services, and the churches seem to be constantly in use. The Boston
churches are used on an average of four nights each week. In
addition, the Beta church makes its facilities available to others;
for example, a local Gospel choir uses the building for practice,
although none of its members belongs to the Beta congregation.
Because the congregations consist mostly of working people, the
buildings are not often used during the daytime.[3] There have
been recurrent attempts to hold a noonday prayer service, but
turnout has been poor and this service has been discontinued.

Each congregation has basically the same services, built from
a set of basic elements. Services are distinguished mainly by the
varying combinations of these elements and by the purposes for
which they are held. Thus, the Sunday morning and evening services are identical as to order of worship, the main distinction
being that the morning service has no testimony segment.

Active members of the congregations attend services three or

2. The week is the liturgical unit of the Mount Calvary churches. There
are not the seasonal divisions found in Catholicism or any theologically
or religiously significant cycle longer than the weekly one. There is a
yearly cycle of meetings and convocations, but this cycle has no religious
significance. There is also a practice of having revivals in the fall, usually for the support of the winter fuel fund (the Beta church spent
$4,000–$5,000 in 1972 for heating alone).
3. There have been continuing efforts to utilize the large facilities of the
Beta church for a day-care and community senior citizens' program. This
is consistent with the sentiments of the founder, who was particularly
concerned about these groups. Thus far, however, these efforts have not
been fruitful, due in part to the complexity of the federal funding bu-
reaucracy. If successful, such programs would mean that the building
would be utilized in the daytime, and they would doubtless help to defray the church's heavy maintenance costs, especially heating bills.

four times each week: Sunday morning and, often, evening services, as well as two other services during the week. Each person has his own pattern of attendance, depending on work schedules, family obligations, and energy. "Every Sunday with the children —mostly the morning and, if I can make it, the evening service. I attend prayer meetings when I can make it, because off and on I work nights, too. The Bible class I try to make every Tuesday night."

Four basic activities take place each week: Sunday School, Sunday morning service, Bible class, and prayer meeting. The Sunday School is not a service but a combined Scripture, religious, and moral education class. It precedes the regular Sunday morning service and is geared to involve the whole church. People are divided into age-graded groups with a teacher assigned to each group. Everyone has a book, and the teachers use a teacher's guide with lesson plans and keyed scriptural readings included. All Mount Calvary churches use the *Light and Life* series, which is also used by a number of other churches nationally.[4] The number of people who attend Sunday School varies with the size of the membership, their ages, and the vitality of the Sunday School itself. At Alpha church, attendance is between fifteen and twenty-five. There are four divisions in the Sunday School: young children (nine and under), preteens, teenagers, and adults. When attendance is low, sections may be combined, for example, teenagers with adults. The classes usually run for an hour and a half, with a break during which the youngsters play and go to the candy stores for soft drinks and sweets. The Sunday morning service follows at eleven o'clock. The Sunday Schools at the other two churches operate similarly. Attendance figures for Beta church are much higher because of the larger membership, and those for Gamma are slightly lower.[5]

4. Lyle E. Williams, ed., *Light and Life* (Winona Lake, Ind.: Light and Life Press). The lessons are based on *International Sunday School Lessons,* International Bible Lessons for Christian Teaching (1970).
5. The pastor of Beta church said that there were about 106 enrolled in the Sunday School and that two thirds of that number attended regularly. Members of that congregation, however, disputed both figures and

The regular Sunday morning service is the major service for the week. Those who are not active in the church will attend this service, if they attend at all: "and on Sunday morning, you get mostly all of them. Don't see them no more till next Sunday morning—that's the way it is." Sunday morning is the archetype of the services. Most other services follow the pattern of Sunday morning, the only difference being that other services may have a testimony segment. The service has three basic parts: a "devotional service," a "service of the Word," and a closing. The devotional service includes hymns, a prayer, and a Scripture reading. The service of the Word begins with the offerings, followed by hymn selections from the choir. (This order is often reversed, however, with the pastor calling upon the choir when he takes over after the devotional service. The former approach allows the spiritually edifying segments of the service to go forward without interruptions for mundane business. A similar concern sometimes leads to the postponing of the offerings until after the "message" and altar call.) After the offerings and hymns, there is then the "message," and this segment often concludes with an altar call; the closing includes announcements (unless they were given during the devotional part of the service), recognition of visitors, and opportunities for others "to have words," that is, to offer brief comments. The Sunday afternoon and evening services are copies of this morning service, with the addition of the "testimony service."

The Bible class, which meets on Tuesday evening at Alpha and on Thursday evening at the other two churches, is simply that.[6] A group gathers to study the Scriptures. A teacher, usually the pastor, guides the reading and supplies commentary as to

argued that attendance was poor due to the ineffectiveness of the Sunday School.

6. There was some dispute about the Bible class at Beta, the pastor claiming that it was active and vital and several members claiming otherwise: "No, they don't have a Bible class now. Tuesday night is Pastor's Aid. Thursday night is prayer meeting, everything mixed up, a regular service. Sometimes we have preaching, most times she teaches, gives her a chance to answer questions."

meaning and historical details that are important to an understanding of the texts. The church generally uses the King James
Version, but there is great variety in the editions used. The
classes are fairly small and are attended mainly by adults and
those seeking "to get deeper in the Lord."

The prayer meeting is a service held on Thursday evening at
Alpha and on Tuesday evening at Gamma church. It is not clear
when the Beta church holds its prayer meeting or whether they
have a separate service for it. The prayer service is basically a
round; the pastor usually leads off or designates someone to begin, and each person in the group who so desires—or is asked—
prays publicly. The rest of the congregation loudly affirms the
sentiments of the one praying, and the spirit is often "high" at
these services. When all have finished, the pastor makes some
comments, and then all are dismissed. The prayer meeting is
usually preceded by an opening hymn and a Scripture reading.
Attendance at this service is also rather small, again mainly
adults; young people do not appear especially interested in this
service. Those who attend are usually among the more active and
zealous members of the congregations.

A number of other liturgical observances are of secondary importance in the day-to-day life of the churches—baptisms, weddings, ordinations—or are relatively infrequent in observance—
Communion service (in Beta church), revivals.

Revivals are a special case and are important to the churches
in two ways: as potential money-raising mechanisms and, more
importantly, as vehicles for bringing new ideas and members
into church. These functions are not, however, currently being
fulfilled. In the past, the Beta church utilized one of its wings
as a revival center and realized income from the proceeds of the
revivals (which presumably more than offset the cost of heat and
maintenance of the building). This was also true of the Alpha
church: "I had Bishop ——— and we split it 60/40—60 for
him, 40 for the church, and he gets all the envelopes. We did
pretty good but still wasn't nothing to brag about. After Reverend Ike came, I know we raised over thousands of dollars."

At the present time, revivals are declining in popularity. The community does not turn out en masse, as it did in the past. Revivals seem to be more for the "edification of the saints" than for the "saving of souls." The unsaved do not come in large numbers; with smaller audiences, the offerings are smaller and new members are not so easily recruited into the church. One member noted:

I remember when we first started, even when I first started traveling with Dad (Bishop Johnson), Oh, the revivals we used to have were something. Souls would be blessed by the hundreds. Now it seems that people have fallen away from revivals and only once in a while do you hear of a good revival. But during that time, revivals were it . . . like in the thirties and forties, all Dad had to do was announce that he was going to be there and if you weren't there at six o'clock, you couldn't even get in the church. Even all out in the yard, people would be there. But now things have really changed. You know, you can have a revival and just the faithful few will attend. . . . People are not so anxious to go to church now; they would rather go to the beach or anywhere instead of coming to church—or sit down and look at TV or listen to the radio. To me it's a falling away. It's not as good as it was in those days.

The declining attendance at revivals increases the financial burden on the few who continue to be active in the church. Not only must they continue to lend visible support to the service, but they are obliged to increase their giving to make up for those who do not appear. As a consequence, the churches try to schedule revivals so that the members of other churches can attend and lend their support. This effort is not always successful, and during the fall and winter months it seems at times that the churches are constantly "in revival." [7] A widely known evangelist—for example, the "Reverend Ike" referred to above or the Reverend Arturo Skinner—can still "pack out" a church. Except for such

7. A number of members objected to what they saw as a constant round of services. They felt that there were far too many services, that members were overburdened with supporting them, and, in a few cases, that there were other things people should be doing besides going to church all the time.

figures, however, revivals are small-scale and strictly limited operations. They continue to be important as fund-raising activities, whether they are successful in soul-saving terms or not. Beta church, for example, has a revival each fall to raise funds for its winter heating bill. Moreover, because revivals are usually "preached" by visiting clergy, often out-of-towners, those attending are exposed to different viewpoints, and local ministers pick up new ideas for their own later use: "I hope you all took out your notebooks now. There were a lot of good ideas there. I know I got meat for several sermons tonight." [8]

The Communion service is also important for the churches. At the Alpha and Gamma churches, it is held on the first Sunday of each month; Alpha has its service on Sunday evening, and at Gamma Communion follows the morning service. The Beta church does not have a regularized Communion service.[9] The pre-Communion service is variable; in some cases, a regular service is held, whereas others follow a much abbreviated ritual. The Communion itself, however, is a commemorative and not a sacramental meal. As with Methodists, grape juice and matzoth are used. The account of the Last Supper in Matthew's Gospel is usually read, and the juice and matzoth are distributed and consumed at the appropriate places in the narrative. After the "meal," the service is quickly dismissed. Even when only a Communion service is held, a large attendance gathers, due in part to strong feelings engendered by the Communion symbolism. At Alpha, ten or more usually attend; at Beta, there is also quite a large number, partly because Beta has Communion in conjunction with other services but also because in the past the founder, Bishop Johnson, often celebrated the service and the strong personal attachments to him increased the turnout.

8. A bishop's comment to the other ministers present after an interesting sermon at a special service at Beta church.
9. Beta church offers Communion several times during the year, and occasionally with foot washing—for example, on Holy Thursday—before Communion. The pastor said that the founder did not want them to have Communion too often because he felt that then it would not be so meaningful.

Order of Service

Protestantism generally lacks the liturgical variety of Catholicism, and churches within the Pentecostal tradition are no exception. Within the Mount Calvary churches there is one basic liturgical model, which is used for most services other than Communion, wedding ceremonies, and so on. This model is laid out here and discussed in archetypal form. There are variations among the three congregations, but the structure is basically the same; on those occasions when the three congregations gather, all follow the same order without difficulty. The archetypal service is ordered thus:

Devotional service

1. Opening song(s)
2. Scripture reading
3. Requests for prayer
4. Prayer
5. Song service
6. Testimony service

The Service of the Word

7. Offering(s)
8. Choir selection(s)
9. Sermon
10. Altar call

Closing

11. Announcements and recognition of visitors
12. Benediction and dismissal

The major subsegments are the song and Testimony services, the sermon, and the altar call. The offerings are not very important in terms of ritual dynamics, but they are crucial elements of the service and important for obvious reasons. The other items are more nearly secondary in terms of the service dynamics.

DEVOTIONAL SERVICE. 1. The opening song is the usual convention for opening the service. It is usually begun by the devotional leader but may be initiated by other members of the congregation. No specific hymn is used. The start of the hymn is the signal for people to stop chatting and to settle down to the business at hand, namely, the service. Usually, a single hymn is sung at this time, but there may be two or three, depending on the wishes of the devotional leader. If there are only a few people in the church but many more are expected, or if the service has begun on time rather than being delayed, there may be two or more opening hymns as latecomers straggle in.

2. A Scripture reading follows the hymn(s). Generally, a few verses of Scripture are read by the devotional leader or the person designated by him to do so. There is no set verse; the reader is free to choose which verses he will read. The most common readings are from the Book of Psalms.

3-4. After the Scripture reading another hymn is sung, and then members of the congregation announce their prayer requests. Sometimes these are specific (for example, for a loved one, for someone ill, or for some other special intention), but they are as often formularized: "I ask the prayers of the saints tonight for the service, for the speaker of the hour, for our pastor and church, for my family, especially my sister, who went to the doctor Tuesday and he told her she had to have an operation." After the various requests are heard, a public prayer is said, generally by the devotional leader or by someone designated by him. In such cases, persons are advised beforehand that they will be asked to read or pray and will thus have an opportunity to prepare. This prayer is a public and social one. The person praying leaves out his or her personal intentions and prays for those of the collectivity—the service, the pastor, the church, the speaker of the hour, the sick, the Mount Calvary churches generally, and so forth. A hymn is often softly hummed as background prior to and during the prayer. The following prayer had begun to the accompaniment of "I Need Thee, oh, I need Thee":

My heavenly Father, again we thank Thee for the privilege of gathering at Thy feet. We thank Thee, Lord, for the writer says, "We need Thee every hour." This afternoon we thank Thee for Thy presence.

We thank Thee for open doors. ["Yes, Lord."] Tonight, Lord, we beg Thy blessings upon our service in Jesus' name. O Lord, look down in mercy upon us, bless our pastor and our bishop tonight, Lord, we pray. Bless, O Lord, the speaker of the hour. We pray that Thou would anoint her lips tonight [*affirmation*] in Jesus' mighty name, O Lord. Honor the unspoken requests tonight, Lord; honor the spoken ones tonight, Lord. O Lord, you know them all by name and by nature, Lord [*rising crescendo of affirmation*], you know their needs tonight, Lord [*chorus of clapping and "Yes, Lord"*]. You know their sufferings tonight, Lord. We pray that Thou would touch, Lord, and heal by Thy Word, we pray, Lord. Tonight we thank Thee for Thy goodness, we thank Thee for Thy love, Lord, we thank Thee because the Word of God says: "The hands of the Lord are upon the righteous," as we cry unto Thee, Lord. We pray that Thou wouldst bless us, Lord, in Jesus' name we pray and Christ is the Savior.

Public prayers like this are often accompanied by vigorous vocal and hand-clapping responses. These responses serve as audience affirmations of the speaker's sentiments; they punctuate the spaces between the speaker's phrases and are often vocalized along with his praying.

5. After the prayer, the devotional leader(s) opens the song service. A hymn is intoned and the accompanist and congregation join in, with the accompanist taking the key from the person who intoned the hymn. The song service is an early part of the service devoted to congregational singing and "is given to them [the congregation] for their participation." [10] The devotional leader(s) compiles a list of hymns to be sung. The number of hymns and the length of the song service are determined by the overall length of the service and thus vary. On a week-night when there is a late start, there will be few hymns. At a Friday or Saturday night revival, when people do not have to work the next day and can afford to spend more time in church, there may be as many as five hymns. In such cases, the song service becomes a community sing; people may "shout" and "get happy" during this part of the service.[11]

10. Interview with the pastor of Beta church.
11. There are often two accompanists in a church, a pianist and an or-

The corpus of hymns is large. Beta church has recently begun using the official *Methodist Hymnal*,[12] and the other two churches use similar, although not identical, collections. The corpus is not limited, however, to standard hymns;[13] rather, a large body of hymns from the oral tradition and southern background of the members provides the basis of the congregations' repertory. A relatively small number of hymns predominate in frequency, depending on a congregation's devotional leader.[14] It is the devotional leader who chooses the hymns, and his or her preferences are naturally reflected in what is sung at the services. In Mount Calvary churches, hymns are usually syncopated and played at a medium tempo, a pace that helps to get people in the mood—comfortably "in the groove"—for the rest of the service. A run of hymns at a fast tempo would tire people, whereas too many slow ones would make them restless. The devotional leader's selection thus requires some care. Comments are often added that reflect upon and unify the hymns. After the hymn, "He's Sweet, I Know," one pastor commented: "Yes, He's sweet, I know,

ganist. Both Alpha and Gamma are limited to one keyboard accompanist; Alpha does not have an organ. There seem to be few restrictions on the instrumentation allowed; drums and electric guitars have become common, although not in the three Boston congregations. Visiting churches bring their own additional instrumentation, choirs, and accompanists.

12. *The Methodist Hymnal* (Baltimore: Methodist Publishers, 1939).

13. The standard hymns that are used are done much differently than they are written in the hymnals, especially in matters of accent, rhythm, and key. Hymnals are used primarily for the words and melody line. For the most part, hymns are transliterated into a Gospel mode.

14. Among the most popular are: "You Don't Know Like I Know," "Down at the Cross," "Jesus, Keep Me near the Cross," "Glory, Glory Hallelujah since I Laid My Burdens Down," "Oh, How I Love Jesus," "Higher Ground," "I Get Joy When I Think about. . . ." Pope (*Millhands and Preachers*, p. 90) lists favorite hymns of churchgoers in Gastonia, North Carolina, several of which are also popular in the Mount Calvary Boston churches. Because Pope is speaking of White Baptist and Methodist and not Holiness or Pentecostal churches, these hymns are presumably of traditional folk origin and appeal across denominational lines.

and I'll tell the world that I've found a Savior. ("Yes, Lord.")
And He's sweet, I know. I heard a writer say, 'He first loved me
and He died to set me free.' Won't you join with me and sing that
song, 'Oh, How I Love Jesus' in your song books?" During the
song service, the congregation sometimes gets into the spirit of
things and takes off on its own, continuing to sing a particularly
rousing hymn. When this happens, the leader allows the popular
will its head for a chorus or two, then reasserts control and
moves on.

6. The testimony service follows the song service and is introduced by the devotional leader with a formula such as "We
will now open our service for testimony." In this part of the
service, the congregation has its say. Each member has the opportunity to get up and "preach" a little if so inclined. Members
"testify to the goodness of the Lord"—that is, they tell what He
has done for them—for the edification and encouragement of
one another and "to [publicly] give God the praise." The testimony is conventionalized and follows a basic three-step pattern:
one person begins his or her testimony with a hymn; the congregation joins in for a verse or two, occasionally for the entire
hymn; then the person who has led off and is already standing
gives his or her testimony.[15] The basic pattern is generally ad-
hered to: an acknowledgment of the Almighty and various persons present or absent; a recounting of the instances of the Lord's
blessing for which the person is thankful (deliverance from personal or financial problems, ill health, spiritual and emotional
trials, and so on); and a conventionalized conclusion requesting
the continued prayers of the saints for the person who is testifying ("I ask all those who know the words of prayer to continue

15. The hymn at the beginning of Testimony is not a Mount Calvary
practice. It is a standard way of testifying in other Pentecostal churches
and was the practice in the United Holy Church. The founder of Mount
Calvary, Bishop Johnson, did away with the practice, however. He did
not want people to mix song with their testimony. Visitors are allowed
to testify in their usual manner, although members have been corrected
for beginning their testimony with song. Since the founder's death, however, the practice is gradually falling into disuse.

to pray my strength in the Lord." When finished, the testifier sits down, and another rises to repeat the process; if there is a lull, testimony may be encouraged by the devotional leader(s) or the pastor. Two examples of testimony follow. The first is taken from a completely conventionalized testimony in which the person testifying does not interject particular personal references; the second is more personal.

I give honor to the Spirit of the Lord this afternoon and to my bishop and pastor, to Reverend ———, to Reverend ———, to Deacon ———, and to all the missionaries, saints, and friends. I'm thankful to the Lord for waking me up this morning still clothed in my right mind, with the activities of my limbs and the blood still running warm in my veins. He didn't have to do it but He did, and for that I'm thanking Him this evening, and I pray that I will continue to praise Him more and more. And I ask all to continue to pray much for me that I will be the daughter that He is looking for in these last and evil days.

I give honor to my Lord and Savior, Jesus Christ, to our overseer ———, to our pastor ———, to all the ministers of the Gospel, to all the saints and friends. I honor the Lord for His loving kindness and tender mercies. Truly I can say today that the Lord is good and His mercies endure forever. You know, I just thank the Lord for all His goodness to me because as the song says, "When I think of the goodness of Jesus and all He's done for me, my very soul cries out, Hallelujah!" I praise the Lord for how He's touched me. And today I can say that the Lord has really blessed me and I'm so glad. . . . I cannot help but thank the Lord each time that I get up from home. He blessed me and brought me through with my operation, because I realize that some were there in the hospital and they didn't make it, but I'm so happy about it. It's so wonderful when you put your trust in the Lord, because He said He will never leave you or forsake you. You know, tonight—I'm a witness tonight that the Lord will do just as He said. You know, I feel so good way down in my soul, and I want you to pray for me that the will of the Lord might be wrought in my life and that I might be a soldier for Him. Pray my strength in the Lord.

Both examples are typical. Although the latter is much longer than the former, it is not unusually so. Some people are particularly blessed or especially moved to "tell it" in great detail. Thus, testimonies vary greatly in length from the perfunctory to the five-to-seven-minute range. When they are too long, the congregation will fidget and shows its restlessness, but this is generally the limit of sanctions invoked if a person takes advantage of the congregation's tolerance. After such a testimony is finished, however, the devotional leader may imply criticism by asking the congregation not to make testimonies too long. Everyone is encouraged to testify, and most do so. Some people do it "better" than others, and although there is no conscious ranking of testimony givers some are acknowledged to have more wit, style, or interesting things to say than others.[16]

There is a routine for giving testimony, but it is not elaborate or codified. Members have their preferred "slots," and some testify early and others late. This minimal sequential order breaks down, however, in the presence of visitors. A visiting congregation brings its own pattern of testifying; visitors are accustomed to testifying in their own services at a certain point. Thus, when there is a mixed gathering, the normal rhythm of testimony is upset. People rise and find themselves speaking along with one or more others. When this occurs, the main rule is politeness, and people defer to one another. There is no special order, but a layman will generally defer to a cleric. The person who defers waits until the other has finished and then gives his testimony. Congregation size does not seem to limit the amount of testimony, except in the very largest cases. Whether there are few or many, testimony is sought equally, and proportionately, as many testify in both instances. The major constraint is intrinsic to the service and its timing, that is, how long the service is expected to last and what night of the week it is. People may be asked to keep their testimony brief, but that is due to a desire to keep the service moving or a wish "to put the speaker up early." Because of the demography of membership, most testimony givers are middle-aged women. Others testify, but there is a reticence on

16. One informant noted: "I heard Sister ———— testify the other night, and she really gave a sweet testimony. I sure would like to hear her preach."

the part of young people to do so. Ministers in the pulpit generally do not testify. After an appropriate period (depending on the hour, the size of the gathering, and so on), the testimony service is closed with a standardized formula—for example, "If there are no further testimonies, we will now bring this part of our service to a close and will now turn the service into the hands of our pastor." A hymn may also follow the testimony service.

THE SERVICE OF THE WORD. 7. After the devotional service is concluded, those overseeing it "give the service back into the hands of the pulpit." The pastor or one of his assistants takes over at this point. The pastor indeed, often delays his entrance into the sanctuary until just before this, choosing instead to remain in a study or other part of the church in prayer and preparation. When the minister takes over after the Devotional Service, all rise as he comes forward to the rostrum and he may invoke a hymn to signify this turning point in the service. After some introductory comments, the minister will ask that the offerings be taken up. A deacon, church mother, or minister usually "stands for the offering(s)." [17] At a special service, with a visiting congregation, one of the visitors is also asked to stand and "help raise the offering." If there is a guest speaker, two offerings are taken up, one for the church and one for the speaker.[18] At a special service or revival, one of those standing for the offering will set a specific amount to be reached for that service: "All right, saints, I know there aren't but a few of us here tonight, but we want to get fifty dollars. And I'll start it off by giving ten dollars. Here it is [*pause in which the offering is conspicuously placed in the plate*]; now all you have to do is give

17. In addition to the regular church and/or speaker's offering, a missionary offering is also taken up on Sunday mornings to support foreign mission work. Mount Calvary has affiliated churches in Liberia, Nigeria, Barbados, and Jamaica and a medical clinic in Haiti. At the Beta church, there is a "twenty-five cents consecration offering." This does not appear to be budgeted separately, although the pastor said that it is used "for hospitality for guests."

18. The pastor of Beta said, "My members always give me an offering when I speak," and the speaker's offering there is generally the bigger one. This is contrary to Alpha practice.

forty dollars, so come on." Whether or not a specific charge is given, the faithful are exhorted to give generously. They march to the front of the church and place their money in "offering plates" on a table below the rostrum. The table is presided over by those standing for the offering. They count the money and make change for those who have large bills. If the money is sufficient, a prayer is offered by one of those standing, the money is delivered to the secretary, and the service is "turned back into the hands of the pastor/pulpit." (Sometimes at this point but usually near the end of the service, the total collection is announced to the congregation.) Most often the amount collected initially is insufficient; if it is short by a small sum, say, less than a dollar, those standing are expected to make up the difference themselves and round off the amount to the next dollar. This is a factor in making this post unattractive. Those standing must serve initially as an example of liberality and then must give again after everyone else, so the strain on anyone who has to stand frequently is apparent. The amount that must be raised is usually substantial, and the congregation is urged "to dig a little deeper." The exhortation for increased giving demands skill in getting people to part with their money; strategies have been developed by the clergy to get people to give and by the members to keep from giving. In the words of one interviewee, "Just about all of them seem to be trying to find a way to raise money. I think it's recent because it looks like it's harder to get money than before. I remember one time you didn't have to worry about it—took up your offering and people give—but now people hold back so you have to find a way to make people give without going in their pockets and taking it. Half of us don't pay our tithes any more." Members, on the other hand, may leave their pocketbooks at home, absent themselves from the congregation at offering time, or employ other stratagems. A minister who is especially good at "raising offerings" is fond of saying in such a situation: "Don't give till it hurts, give till it helps." Those standing may even "wait on you" to further encourage members to give. After additional money has been collected, it is counted; if still insufficient, the process continues.

Depending on the need of the pastor and church, the collection may be drawn out until the desired amount is obtained.[19] The entire process often takes twenty minutes or more. When the "message" is "brought" by a preacher other than the pastor, a "speaker's offering" is also collected. This is sometimes taken up with the other offerings, but it can be postponed until after the message. Indeed, the whole offering process may be put off until later. After the collection process is completed, the service is "turned back into the hands of the pastor," who thanks the collectors and the congregation and makes a few appropriate comments.

8. At this point, the pastor begins setting the stage for the "message," choosing his words to put people in a receptive frame of mind. His comments may be about the service, the weather, current events—anything he can use to put people at ease. If the pastor is the speaker, he may then ask the choir(s) to sing a selection or two before he begins the sermon. If he is not, he introduces the speaker, who often calls on the choir to help set the mood.[20] If the speaker is a visitor from another church, he may have brought a group from his own congregation along with him. At this point he would ask his own choir members to offer a selection or two.

9. In keeping with the fundamentalist variant of American Protestant tradition, the sermon or "message" is at the center of the service: "Now we reach that part that we've all been waiting for, the most important part of the service. Before you worked for the Lord, now the Lord will work on you through His word and messenger." In discussing sermons, our focal point is their content. Considerations of form and style, though serious and

19. The author has observed up to fifteen dollars raised in this way. There is, however, long-standing criticism of this practice from people, inside and outside the church, who regard this nagging of people for more money as a sign of the "penny-ante" character of Pentecostalism. Needless to say, pastors and members view this entire process from opposite sides.
20. At some services—though not Sunday morning or a revival—a musical program is presented at this time.

interesting in their own right, are of secondary importance for this exercise. It is sufficient to note that each minister has his or her own style, and there is a grammar and rhetoric particular to this southern Black homiletic tradition.[21] Further, the tradition of folk preaching that Albert Raboteau describes among southern slaves is still very much alive within Black churches from that evangelical fundamentalist tradition.[22] Moreover, there were no apparent idioms or idiosyncracies from outside this tradition that were peculiar to the Mount Calvary Boston churches. In terms of form, again, a threefold division suffices: (1) Almost all sermons begin with a prayer on the part of the speaker, who then reads a passage from Scripture and announces the "subject" of the message, often in phrases from the scriptural passage, thus: "We want to call your attention tonight to the tenth chapter of Ezekiel, the tenth verse. 'And when I looked, behold . . . the four had one likeness as if a wheel had been in the midst of a wheel.' We want you to think about a 'wheel in a wheel.' " (2) The subject is then taken, explicated, and expounded upon, with parables and analogies sprinkled throughout the message. (3) After the sermon has climaxed, it is often concluded with an "altar

21. This homiletic language is rich and varied, and its development and stylistic taxonomy deserve a full-scale treatment. Two references in this area are Bruce Rosenberg, *The Art of the American Folk Preacher* (New York: Oxford University Press, 1970); and Charles V. Hamilton, *The Black Preacher in America* (New York: William Morrow, 1972).

22. "The style of the folk sermon, shared by black and white evangelicals, was built on a formulaic structure based on phrases, verses, and whole passages the preacher knew by heart. Characterized by repetition, parallelisms, dramatic use of voice and gesture, and a whole range of oratorical devices, the sermon began with normal conversational prose, then built to a rhythmic cadence, regularly marked by the exclamations of the congregation, and climaxed in a tonal chant accompanied by shouting, singing, and ecstatic behavior. The preacher, who needed considerable skill to master this art, acknowledged not his own craft but, rather, the power of the spirit which struck him and 'set him on fire.' The dynamic pattern of call and response between preacher and people was vital to the progression of the sermon, and unless the spirit roused the congregation to move and shout, the sermon was essentially unsuccessful." Raboteau, *Slave Religion,* pp. 236–37.

call," literally a call to sinners to come to the altar and "accept
Jesus Christ as your personal and in-dwelling Savior." As such,
it is the goal of much of the preaching and the specific end toward which the sermon is directed.

A popular misconception regards churches from the Pentecostal and southern evangelical traditions as preaching strictly
"hellfire and damnation." In the Boston cases, this view is clearly
in error, for the emphasis in preaching is placed on sustaining,
encouraging, and edifying an audience that, by and large, is
already "saved." Even in revivals, the concern these days is more
for the renewal of the saints than for saving the souls of the unchurched. Sermons designed to frighten people are still preached,
but they are far from the norm. Salvation is, however, a prime
concern, and the emphasis in preaching is to make it a most
attractive goal rather than to frighten people with the consequences of sin.

Are you just drifting night after night; are you just sitting Sunday
after Sunday, getting nothing out of the services, getting no joy from
the wells of salvation, getting no strength? What is the meaning of
my life? We ought to ask ourselves this question. Then we ought to
have the conviction that Christ had. "To this end I was born." You
know, some Christians act so much like they're sad they're saved. They
act like, "Oh, if I hadn't gotten in it, I wouldn't!" . . . look like some
married folks. . . . Most married folks will tell you, "Honey, if I had
never gotten in it, I wouldn't now." Say Amen. But isn't the religious
life beautiful! Sweet Jesus, just to take Him at His word, just to rest
upon His promise, and to know the Savior Lord. Hallelujah! Hallelujah! Our fight is over. We've found Him and we're glad, we'll never
more be sad. Since the Savior found us, He's put His arms around us.
Glory to God! We will help the searchers, but we're not searching
any more . . . . I heard the writer of a song say, "I never knew joy till
I met the Lord." Wherever you meet God, you meet joy, you meet
sunshine, you meet durability, you meet stability. You've never known
joy till you've met the Lord.

Sermons are also designed to educate the congregation. Because most members attend church only on Sunday, the educative
function of the sermon is an important one. This function is not

as crucial as in Catholicism, however, where the only religious exposure the vast majority of adult Catholics get is at Sunday mass. In Pentecostal churches generally, and in Mount Calvary churches in particular, the level of specifically religious commitment is very high; many people have a habit of Bible reading and independent study and are exposed to a religious framework outside of church. Thus, they are more likely than Catholics, for example, to receive religious "reinforcement" outside of church services. Further, preaching is usually biblically based, and an effort is made to forge links between the Book and the contemporary lives of the congregation. There is thus a dynamic, ongoing interpretative effort to maintain the vitality and applicability of the Scriptures to daily life.

Now listen, in the space of time this good man came back to investigate what those men had done; and the one He gave ten talents, he went to work and gained five talents; and the one He gave two talents had gained two others; and the one He gave one talent, he couldn't trust God because of that he didn't get enough. "I'll bury it," he said. You know, a lot of people are like that today, they haven't changed. You give them five of something, they're going to spend it, they won't even invest it in anything you have. If they put money in your business, they want to run it.

Nor is this interpretative effort limited to sermons; it is integral to the life of the church and to the lives of many of the members. There is a continuing meditation on the Book and a re-working of its application to the present, both in preaching and in the Bible class. This practice in the churches has a greater impact on the active members, those who attend an average of three or more services each week; because most services have a "message" as component, these members receive continuous doses of this biblical reflection.

As noted earlier, although people in these churches are not frightened into heaven, salvation remains a major concern. This is especially true at revivals and other large services where there are likely to be "unsaved" persons. In bringing about conversion or, more accurately, getting the "unsaved" and the backsliders "to claim their salvation" by "acknowledging Jesus Christ as their personal and in-dwelling Savior," the ambience and dynamics of the service become important. The "emotionalism" that numerous observers have noted in Pentecostal services has a specific place here. The enthusiasm and active response and participation of the congregation coupled with the "powerful preaching" of the minister create a charged situation. Enormous pressures are generated on the sinner and the unchurched. They have usually been raised in the church or under its influence, and they know and understand the world as defined therein. They may have withdrawn their assent but not their conviction of the efficacy of the church and, more important, its claim to truth (otherwise, they would not bother to come to church). Thus, their prior conviction, the social pressures generated by the ambience of enthusiasm, and their sense of guilt often combine to literally force assent to the altar call when it is made. "I was on my way out the door, when something seized me and forced me back up the aisle to the altar."

This group dynamic and its power are known but are not acknowledged in such bald terms. A preacher may indicate on occasion that special prayers are requested so that some person will be "saved" during the service. This is viewed as "putting the Lord on them." It is not acknowledged that it is also putting the congregation on them.[23]

10. The altar call follows the conclusion of the sermon. It is the opportunity given to the "unsaved" to come forward to be saved and "to acknowledge Jesus as your personal and in-dwelling savior." As noted, there are enormous pressures generated upon the "sinner," and they are focused at this particular point in the service. The sinner's status may not be publicly known,

23. At the 1972 Massachusetts State Convocation, a long-lost brother of the Beta church pastor came to the Sunday morning service. She announced his presence to the congregation, told how he had been feared lost, how he had called her the night before and promised to come to church the next morning. She then singled him out of the congregation and said that she was going to pray "that the Lord would save him and add him to the rolls of that church and that before he left the church that day he'd be saved." His being saved under such immense social pressure was not surprising.

but his own knowledge and his awareness that *God knows* are enough to make the congregation's expectations (and enthusiastic longing for his salvation) extremely difficult to resist.[24] Some are able to resist, and "sinners" will avoid certain preachers because they fear "being convicted" under their preaching and having to give up their sinful lives. It is also potentially very embarrassing to have to come forward during an altar call, for it means openly admitting to being unsaved or to having fallen away. People no longer live in the closeness of southern small towns, and the anonymity of northern big-city life is much to the advantage of the sinner. He can sit in the congregation, and even his identity may be unknown to most. Of course, the condition of his soul under these circumstances can be a secret between him and the Almighty. To have to be convicted of sin under such circumstances is to willingly step into the spotlight of congregational attention. A great many people quail before such a step.

During the altar call, the ambience is kept at a highly charged level through the words of the evangelist, the musical accompaniment, and other devices, all of which "keep the pressure up." While the service is at this high pitch, individuals may be moved to shout. What appears to happen is that some can take the pressure only so long and then are moved by it to demonstration. Most often, women will "shout" or collapse in response to the charged atmosphere. These personal demonstrations serve to increase the tension of the service, particularly when a number of people are "falling out." This "overflow" of enthusiasm during some altar calls is distinct from that which often follows the sermon, when people, giving vent to the spirit, "shout" for joy. The response during the altar call, though identical in form, is different in function. It helps maintain the pressure on the "un-

24. A member testified how she came to be saved. She had gone to service, and the preacher knew of her and her "unsaved" condition. The altar call was kept open so long that "I decided that I might as well go on up there and get saved so we can go home." There was much laughter over the story, but it aptly illustrated some of the social dynamics of "getting saved."

saved"; both give vent to ecstasy and enthusiasm, but the "over-flow" after the sermon helps to "cool" things off, whereas that during the altar call "keeps the heat up."

After a successful altar call, the preacher converses with and prays over those persons newly "saved" and then has them testify. They will often "shout" while being prayed over and may require restraint; when they testify, they tell how wonderful they feel, how they have now come to a personal knowledge of Jesus, and how they are going to stay close to Him now, and they ask the prayers of the congregation for themselves.

During revivals, there is always a prayer and healing service after the altar call. The pattern is similar to an altar call: People are invited to come forward with their requests for prayer and healing. In contrast to the altar call, people readily come forward during the healing service. All are in need of prayer or have bodily ills of which they wish to be relieved. Seeking relief here is not embarrassing, as coming forward during the altar call would be: Responding to the altar call is a public admission before all church members of one's sinful condition, whereas everyone stands in need of prayer and healing. During the prayer and healing service, people come forward and discuss their particular ills and needs with the minister, who lays hands upon the supplicant while praying over him or her. The prayers may vary, depending on the preacher and the person being prayed over. "O God, we come before you this evening; heal your faithful servant, O God. Rebuke this ill, O Lord; deliver her from this affliction. Heal this backache; make her every whit whole. We ask in Jesus' name. Amen."

CLOSING. 11. After the prayer and healing service is concluded, the preacher returns to the pulpit and turns the service over to someone else, usually another minister, who "has words" that help to calm the mood if the "Spirit is still high." The ministerial role at this point is that of a master of ceremonies; he calls upon other ministers to "have words" and acknowledges visitors. If the announcements of upcoming church events have not been given previously they are given at this point. On the last night of a revival or at a special service, a "vote of thanks" is given at the end of the announcements. Someone from the auxiliary that sponsored the service or an individual designated by the pastor thanks the preacher and visiting church for attending and offers the host church's assistance to the visitors.

12. When everything has been said, the service is turned back to the preacher for the benediction and dismissal. Each minister has his or her own formulas: "If there are no further announcements, I will now turn the service back into the hands of the speaker for the last say and dismiss." The preacher comes forward and raises his hands or arms, the members of the congregation raise one or both of theirs, and the preacher says: "Grace, mercy, and truth, from God the Father, through Jesus Christ, the Son of the Father, with the Holy Spirit, in peace and love, let the church say Amen." At this point, the service is concluded. The ministers and congregation gather round to greet each other, shaking hands, congratulating the speaker on his sermon. There is often laughter and mirth. People visit and exchange news. In Mount Calvary churches after the service, people hug and kiss each other in greeting and affection.

This practice is limited, however, to the adults. Teenagers play the usual adolescent games; young people gather on the church steps to talk and flirt while the adults are still visiting inside. Depending on the time and the day or night of the week, some may go to a nearby restaurant for a snack and continue visiting.[25] For the most part, this is the extent of extrareligious fellowship.

People rarely return home from a night service before 10:30 or 11:00. Those who work the night shift leave just before or just after the sermon in order to be at work on time; most of those, however, do not bother to come to church when they must work unless there is a special occasion, such as the last night of a revival or the presence of the senior bishop. The bulk of the congregation stays until the end of the service.

This is the basic order of the Mount Calvary service in Boston. It is characteristic of Sunday morning, Sunday afternoon, and

25. This is truer of Alpha than of Beta. Beta church tends to get out later, and the congregation thus has less time to go out after the service.

evening services and also of special services and revivals. Sunday School and prayer services proceed somewhat differently, as does the Communion service, although it is usually preceded by a regular service. The remainder of Mount Calvary rituals (baptisms, ordinations, funerals, and so on) are irregular in occurrence, shorter, and more pointed in their purpose. Furthermore, they sometimes take place within the context of regular services, particularly in the case of the ordination of deacons.

Roles in the Service

This straightforward content analysis of service elements is not the only way to describe the ritual life of churches. Religious life has often been discussed in terms of theatrical metaphors. Such a perspective casts a different light on the activities we are examining and gives us answers to a different set of questions than those originally posed. Assuming, then, a dramaturgical framework for the discussion of ritual practice, we can ask what roles are essential to religious performance. There are four necessary role sets.[26] The role of the congregation is first in importance because it is the congregation, by its participation in the ritual(s), that is both creator and consumer of the ritual performance. The congregation is both actor and audience, creating and enjoying the sacred drama by and for itself.[27] The second

26. "The institution with its assemblage of 'programmed' actions, is like the unwritten libretto of a drama. The realization of the drama depends upon the reiterated performance of its prescribed roles by living actors. The actors embody the roles and actualize the drama by representing it on the given stage. Neither drama nor institution exist empirically apart from this recurrent realization." Peter S. Berger and Thomas H. Luckmann, *The Social Construction of Reality* (New York: Doubleday, Anchor Press, 1967), p. 75.

27. Parts of this discussion may be criticized as bordering on theology. It must be noted, therefore, that there is no necessary contradiction between theology and social analysis. Because one of the tasks of theology is inquiry into the relation between man and God and because that relation takes place within history and is by definition social (with pietized and privatistic exceptions), statements about the relation between God and man are sociological analyses of and prescriptions for relations

role set, which includes managerial and performance functions, is almost as important as that played by the congregation as a whole. These roles are usually played by assisting ministers and deacons, church mothers, and the like, although they can be performed by regular members of the congregation as well. They involve such roles as devotional leaders, pulpit ministers who serve as masters of ceremonies after the devotional leaders have finished, commentators who speak after the sermon, and so on. The division of labor for this second set of roles can be extensive, depending on the size of the gathering, but usually these roles are concentrated in one or two hands. The third role set is occupied by the preacher and the "message." This is the central part of the service and the end toward which the ritual process is oriented. It is not simply the province of a single actor—the preacher—who "brings the message" but a collaborative effort between the preacher and the congregation. The fourth set of roles are primarily maintenance functions, generally involving no independent performance but necessary for the ongoing maintenance of the service. They are service necessities, ushers and nurses, musicians, and so on. These are the basic roles that make up the service.

Several writers have at this point sought links between Afro-American and African religious forms.[28] They have noted the similarities between African and Afro-American music and rhythmic patterns. Raboteau, for one, takes special note of these[29]

among men as well as theological positions. Thus, a social analysis that sees the role of the congregation within ritual as primary, as opposed to that of the priest, is also a theological position that has historically gone under the rubric of Congregationalism.

28. Harold Courlander, *Negro Folk Music, U.S.A.* (New York: Columbia University Press, 1963); Herskovits, *Myth of the Negro Past*; Allan Lomax, *Folk Song, U.S.A.* (New York: Duell, Sloan, and Pearce, 1947).

29. "The singing style of the slaves, which was influenced by their African heritage, was characterized by a strong emphasis on call and response, polyrhythms, syncopation, ornamentation, slides from one note to another, and repetition. Other stylistic features included body movement, hand-clapping, foot-tapping and heterophony." Raboteau, *Slave Religion*, p. 74.

and, in addition, focuses on the collective creation of ritual performance engaged in by the congregation on the one hand and indigenous Africans performing native rites on the other.

> In the ring shout and allied patterns of ecstatic behavior, the African heritage of dance found expression in the evangelical religion of the American slaves. . . . similar patterns of response—rhythmic clapping, ring-dancing, styles of singing, all of which result in or from the state of possession trance—reveal the slaves' African religious background. . . . If, as Payne claims, the "ignorant masses" [read, "less acculturated"] regarded the ring shout "as the essence of religion," and if the shout leader's contention that "without a ring sinners won't get converted" was representative of general belief, the "holy dance" of the shout may very well have been a two-way bridge connecting the core of West African religions—possession by the gods—to the core of evangelical Protestantism-experience of conversion.[30]

The issue of African survivals remains fraught with controversy. There are, however, connections to be made between Black religion and more contemporary forms of Black life. It would seem, for example, that equally useful parallels can be drawn between the dramatic performance created by church congregations on the one hand and by a band of jazz musicians on the other. The band, like the congregation, creates its performance as a collective enterprise. It performs both as a whole—in ensemble—and in several voices—as sections, as soloists. The band has performers who function at times as stage managers, controlling and directing the pace and flow of action. Bands also have performers of maintenance functions, for example, rhythm sections, whose roles directly parallel those of musicians at church services. They provide the accompanying rhythmic patterns by which the creative effort moves. As in the service, these section men, especially in a large aggregation, rarely carry a major solo voice. Their roles as supporting players are too involved in the maintenance of the ongoing performance to allow them much solo role prominence.

A band's efforts collectively and sectionally interlock around

30. Ibid., pp. 72–73.

the composition, integrating the individual solos into a unified whole. At their most vital, these efforts transcend the limits of the score and the shortcomings of individual players, and the performance as a collective creation soars. Such a performance, like the church service, is a collaboration of all the participants: composer, soloists, sidemen, all melding their efforts into a complex unity. As in church, the band has "stars" and major solo voices, but they are dependent on the support and cooperation of the ensemble in order to create good music. If the rhythmic patterns and vocal styles of Africa have reemerged in Afro-American religious guise, despite separation by an ocean and a few centuries, it would seem likely that the striving for transcendent experience and collective creation central to the Afro-American religious tradition would be a key source for jazz's fundamental character as a music of collective creation and improvisation and for the jazzman's concern to continually transcend the limits of form and enter more privileged realms.

The congregation's participation in the service is neither inchoate nor atomized. Rather, it is highly structured into a set of activities defined by individual and group performances. These differentiated activities on the part of the congregation are clearly subordinate and a component of the ritual performance as a holistic endeavor. The congregational singing is clearly a group effort. The testimonies, prayer requests, shouting, speaking in tongues, though performed individually, are available to everyone in the congregation, and everyone has the opportunity to partake in the serial performance of them. It is the total of such activities, not an individual performance such as a single testimony, that constitutes a unit of service.

Another role subsidiary to the congregation is that of the choir and/or the singer(s). At many services, individuals and/or choirs are called upon to "give us a selection or two." These roles are again circumscribed. The people who perform them are primarily congregation members, and they sit in the congregation except when performing as singers (on Sunday morning at Alpha and Beta, they sit in front apart from the congregation). The role is limited to those times when they are called on to sing, usually before the preacher delivers the message. They then take on an identity apart from the congregation but return to their status as congregation members immediately afterward. These individual and group subsidiary roles are not vested in particular persons; their repetition by a rotating "cast" further points up the collective character of the performance.

The second role set involves both managerial and individual performance functions, usually carried out by ministers or deacons.[31] These roles are concentrated for the most part in two persons, the devotional leader and the pastor, who takes over the service after the devotional leader has finished and who performs the service management function, namely, as "master of (sacred) ceremony." For illustration, the infrequent case of a church with a full complement of ministers is useful. In such a case there is a wide division of labor. Each minister has a role to play in the conduct of the service: one may be in charge of the devotional service; another may take over the service as "the hands of the pulpit" after the devotional service is completed; another may be called on to give the altar call, and so on.

The managerial role is more, however, than that of master of ceremonies. It is also a performance role. The person is not simply directing the progress of the service but participating in it. His or her "skill" is of great use in furthering the performance of the service. Thus, the setting of a proper mood when introducing the preacher aids the reception of the message. Again, those "standing for the offering" must be skilled in persuading people to give; if they are insensitive, they may fail to raise the desired amount and may also leave the congregation in a disgruntled mood. This performance aspect is apparent also in the commentaries made after the sermon, when each minister in the pulpit is given the opportunity to "have words." His function is not simply to recapitulate the sermon, but to embellish the topic with a little of his own "fire." He gets the chance to "solo"

31. In the Mount Calvary churches, women often participate in the services on an equal basis with men; the demographics almost necessitate this. Thus, although there are no deaconesses, there are women ministers, and women are as likely to perform these service leadership roles as men.

a bit. It is clear that the managerial and performance functions are not separate in this role.

The same unity of performance and management function is evident in the devotional leaders. Not only do they direct liturgical action, they also participate on an equal level with the congregation. They are more "first among equals" than leaders set apart from the congregation. They testify, sing, and contribute to the ongoing production of the service. The role of devotional leader is, again, not vested in particular individuals but rotated among deacons and members.

These managerial roles are in essence focuses, that is, mechanisms by which the action of the group is directed and channeled. The leaders are truly in charge of activities, but they are not independent. They are more accurately "mouthpieces of the consensus."

The message is the centerpiece of the service; the preacher is central because it is he or she who brings the message.[32] It is in the message that all the elements of the service are focused. In the person and performance of the preacher, the strands of the ritual come together. Through the preacher, the Word is mediated to the faithful in terms meaningful to their lives; through the messenger and the message he delivers, "the Word is made manifest" (*epiphania*). The message brings the religious truth home to the congregation and makes the Almighty real. The performance of the message is a central component in the epiphanies that often occur during the services, one of the functions of strong, powerful preaching being to help people "feel the Spirit," to enable the Spirit "to fall." It is worth reiterating that the messenger does not perform in isolation. The performance of the sermon is a collaboration between the messenger and the congregation. They support and encourage the messenger, offer

32. The preaching role is one that is personalized and vested in particular persons. Ostensibly, one must be ordained to preach. The pastor of the Beta church explained that only ministers may *preach*. Deacons and others not ordained may only *teach*. This distinction does not obtain in practice, as deacons sometimes "bring the message" and missionaries who are not ministers also preach on occasion.

affirmation and comment; he is the mouthpiece of their consensus and the medium by which the Word of the Almighty is mediated to the faithful. Moreover, it is not just the "promptings of the Spirit" but the congregation's active support and participation that inspire his preaching. When the preacher is really preaching, when he is "in gear," "making it right," and the congregation is right with him with encouragement and affirmation, the chemistry of the situation leads to a meeting of God and man in history (*kairos*) through the agency of the Word. Again, there is a close analogy to jazz: When the interplay among the musicians is "right" and the soloists are "really into it," the bounds of technique are transformed, the moment transcended, and the musicians and the audience transported.

The support roles are separate from the congregation, but they are essential nonetheless. The musician's role is an individualized one and is vested in particular persons because of the specific technical skills required. The role is restricted to support of the service so that, although the musicians are in full view, they do not participate in the service as musicians; that is to say, there is no activity that musicians *qua* musicians perform during the service other than producing music. In this sense they are like puppeteers, often in full view of the audience but important only as manipulators of the puppets. What is important about the musicians is their music. Thus, they usually do not testify, make prayer requests, or otherwise participate in the service. Should they wish to testify, they would step out of the musician role and become members of the congregation.

Nurses and ushers provide the other support functions. Their roles are clearly defined and are exercised throughout the service. As with the musicians, these roles are vested in particular persons, and their participation in the service other than in the supportive role is limited. These people tend not to "shout" when serving in these roles (because they are charged with assisting those who get carried away doing so). Although specific persons are ushers or nurses, these are roles anyone can perform; when there are not enough accredited nurses or ushers, other members of the congregation may be pressed into service.

These are the basic roles performed during services. The primacy of the congregation in the performance is clear. Although there is great differentiation in roles, the enterprise is a collective one and, to some extent, the specialized roles are individualized expressions of the congregation and are focuses for the group's expression.[33] Again, the musical analogy seems appropriate. Jazz is also a collective enterprise; there may be stars and soloists, but they are dependent on the support and collaboration of the group to make music. Like the service, the music is a collaborative creation; the individual performer is not independent of others but is part of a larger whole. Again, there is differentiation of roles, but a number of people get a chance to "solo." It is not a question of "stars" being more important than ordinary members of the congregation or band; everyone plays an appointed role in a collective effort to reach the transcendent moment.

The ritual life of the church can therefore be seen not just as routinized worship but as the regular coming together of the congregation to make sacred music and to participate in a ritual drama. There are different (musical) forms or (dramatic) skits for different occasions. Most rituals, however, are drawn from a basic set of components. These components are combined in different ways for different services; some parts may be omitted or different roles may be utilized, but the basic commonality of the rituals and their constituent parts allows everyone to recognize the script or score in use for that evening and to readily find his place in it. This is so even when members gather for fellowship with churches not in the Mount Calvary body.

The large amount of time devoted to the practice of ritual indicates its importance to the life of the church and the lives of its members. More important, this ritual life is constitutive of the

33. This may be one of the meanings of "congregational church organization," where there is not a professional clergy but a "priesthood of all believers." The church is thus not defined apart from its lay members (as is pre-Vatican II Catholicism, where the professional religious were viewed as the church); the body as a whole maintains its identity as the church. Instead of simply attending a particular church, members understand themselves as constituting the church.

church life, for without it the church as it is conventionally known would not exist. Ritual is the common activity that members perform together.

It should be emphasized that, despite descriptions of Black Pentecostal services as chaotic and freewheeling, all services are structured and participants act through their specified roles in constructing the ritual performance.[34] Thus, there is never cacophony; participants always know what "score" is being played that night and what "key" and which "instrumentation" will be used.

These two ways of viewing the ritual life are complementary. The descriptive content analysis of service elements has provided a frame for making sense of the religious action of believers who come out of the Pentecostal–Holiness tradition. The dramaturgical metaphors have made it easier to find connections with other areas of Black expressive life. They suggest, in fact, a fundamental connection between the religious life of Black Americans and jazz, a major musical idiom rooted in their experience. As a form, Mount Calvary ritual practice is the instrumentality for the resurrection of a specifically religious ontology and the means by which the central principle in that ontology is once again made manifest in human history (*epiphania*). It is also the major setting for the encounter of God and man in history (*kairos*), a kairotic moment where sinners can claim their salvation. These are the ends of ritual practice. Its meaning can now be examined.

34. Fauset, *Black Gods;* G. Norman Eddy, "Store-Front Religion," *Religion in Life* 28 (Winter 1958–59): 68–85.

FOUR
Theory and Meaning

One of the tasks of theory is to provide concepts, principles, and points of comparison that can be used in making sense of masses of undigested empirical data. Indeed, theory is supposed to guide not just the interpretation of such data but their initial collection as well. In the case of religion, sociology has produced a large body of literature devoted to this kind of explanatory effort. Faced with the multifarious ways that men are religious, the sociology of religion has sought to understand *why*. What is the meaning of this phenomenon? Unfortunately, much of this effort has turned out to be historically or culturally bound or inadequate to the task.[1]

A more serious criticism of the available theoretical perspectives is that, in attempting to "explain" religion, they explain it away. This has been an especially serious difficulty with a number

---

1. "A great analytical difficulty in the sociology of religion is the extent to which our basic conceptual apparatus is derived from the doctrines of Christian religion. The church–sect distinction developed initially in a sociological context by Weber and Troeltsch is the outstanding specific example of such a 'Christian' conception." Roland Robertson, *The Sociological Interpretation of Religion* (New York: Schocken Books, 1970), p. 43. "These systems of categorization (typologies) are not more than a useful construct for analysis and the available ones have been shown to be culturally and historically bound." Bryan Wilson, *Sects and Society* (London: Heinemann, 1961), p. 7.

of functionalist interpretations.[2] In analyzing religion in terms of its functions in the social order, these interpretations often assume that these functions are sufficient to explain the phenomenon[3] and that they adequately describe its meaning.

Thus, if one proposes that one of the major functions of religion is to reduce anxiety, the argument goes that anxiety causes religion. . . . it would then appear that the sociologist is claiming that anxiety always gives rise to religious commitment of some kind. . . . From a sociological point of view, such arguments are extremely unsatisfactory, since psychological explanations of this kind do not in any way account for the nature of the religious commitment.[4]

The literature on sectarianism under which Pentecostal groups such as Mount Calvary have been generally subsumed exemplifies these problems quite clearly. Wilson asserts, for example:

A sect serves as a small and "deviant" reference-group in which the individual may seek status and prestige and in terms of whose standards he may measure his own talents and accomplishments in more favorable terms than are generally available in the wider society. It alters the context of striving, puts a premium on attributes different from those counted significant in the world, provides the reassurance of a stable, effective society whose commitment and value structure claim divine sanction and divine permanence. Its ideological orientation and its group cohesion provide a context of emotional security

2. "Sect adherence . . . can be meaningfully understood only in terms of psychological and sociological analysis—by reference to actual psychic, social, economic and cultural circumstances—and in terms of the functions which religious belief, affiliation, and activity actually fulfill." Wilson, *Sects and Society*, p. 354. Talcott Parsons does not err in this fashion. See his *Religious Perspectives of College Teaching* (New Haven: Edward Hazen Foundation, n.d.).

3. "Yet, modification of simple socio-economic determinism need not, as some have willingly assumed, impose upon us explanations which presuppose the independent causal significance of religious experience as such. We can seek causal factors in the complexity of social circumstances without being reduced to mysticism or to interpersonal comparisons of the subjective experience of the numinous." Wilson, *Sects and Society*, pp. 5–6.

4. Robertson, *Sociological Interpretation*, pp. 58–59.

so vital to the adherent that its teaching necessarily become for him objectively true.[5]

Wilson's discussion exemplifies the mistaken identity and circularity often hidden in functionalist explanations, which assume an identity between conditions, some of which in fact are prior and others subsequent, both logically and socially. It is because of a person's prior ideological commitment to a faith or belief system that he is a member of the institution within which these beliefs are embodied. It is as a consequence of this logically subsequent affiliation that the social and psychological conditions described above hold. The circularity is evident in that Wilson posits a set of needs in the adherents and then defines the religious group as that which fulfills these posited needs.[6] The intellectual component of religion is also made consequent to the emotional needs of the adherent and, as such, does not have to be dealt with substantively. In this case, the substantive religious question has been virtually "explained away."

Emile Durkheim long ago managed to avoid this particular pitfall in attempting to explain and account for the religious phenomenon in general.

It is readily seen how that group of regularly repeated acts which form the cult get their importance. In fact, whoever has really practiced a religion knows very well that it is the cult which gives rise to these impressions of joy, of interior peace, of serenity, of enthusiasm which are for the believer an experimental proof of his beliefs. The cult is not simply a system of signs by which the faith is outwardly

---

5. Wilson, *Sects and Society*, p. 354.
6. "The fundamental problem has to do with the frequent failure to distinguish between *the conditions which promote religious beliefs and symbols of certain kinds* ... and *the phenomena to which symbols may actually refer*. These two are by no means the same. When we speak of conditions which promote religious beliefs, we, as sociologists and anthropologists, speak of the social experience which constrains individuals to believe in religous phenomena; but this is not to say that the phenomena themselves therefore refer to the experiences. They may, but frequently they do not." Robertson, *Sociological Interpretation*, pp. 155–56.

translated; it is a collection of the means by which this is created and recreated periodically.[7]

Though Durkheim here escapes the circular discussion involving posited needs that ensnared Wilson and focuses instead on the structural dynamics of religious praxis itself—as opposed to the functional conditions of its existence—the substantive question is still obscured in his discussion. Durkheim admits the possibility of the "substantial reality" of which religious experience is the expression: "Our entire study rests upon this postulate that the unanimous sentiment of the believers of all times cannot be purely illusory. Together with a recent apologist of the faith, we admit that these religious beliefs rest upon a specific experience whose demonstrative value is, in one sense, not one bit inferior to that of scientific experiments." [8] It remains for him, however, strictly a logical possibility, not a realistic one.

But from the fact that a "religious experience," if we choose to call it this, does exist and that it has a certain foundation . . . it does not follow that the reality which is its foundation conforms objectively to the idea which believers have of it. Likewise, even if the impressions which the faithful feel are not imaginary, still they are in no way privileged intuitions; there is no reason for believing that they inform us better upon the nature of their object than ordinary sensations upon the nature of bodies and their properties.[9]

Here it becomes clear that for Durkheim, as earlier for Wilson, the world of which religious experience is the sign is not a substantial one. It has no ontological status. Although he asserts the contrary, religion and religious experience, insofar as they do not rest on the ground they claim, are, for him, illusory. "We have seen that this reality, which mythologies have represented under so many different forms, but which is the universal and eternal objective cause of these sensations *sui generis* out of which

7. Emile Durkheim, *The Elementary Forms of the Religious Life* (Glencoe, Ill.: Free Press, 1947), p. 417.
8. Ibid.
9. Ibid., pp. 417–18.

religious experience is made, is society." [10] Durkheim, like Wilson and several other functionalist interpreters, concludes by asserting the ultimate illusory character of religion, although he does so on different grounds. The presumption of the essentially illusory nature of the reality to which religion speaks is a common theme in sociological discussions and is a major stumbling block to an adequate confrontation and understanding of the religious phenomena on *sociological* grounds. One may go right to the point and argue that a determination of the ontological status of the religious world is beyond the methodological capability of sociology. Given this position, however, one must regard the real existence of the supernal religious world as moot and therefore beyond the limits of social science determination. In such a case, the believer's definition of the situation must be dealt with fairly and openly. Unless a theoretical perspective takes seriously the world or definition of reality (and *Weltanschauung*) of the groups with which it deals and which it attempts to understand, it will invariably misunderstand or, worse, debunk the world religious believers inhabit and, in doing so, will debunk the believers as well.

The literature on sectarianism manifests in microcosm the problems we have been examining in the more general social theoretical perspectives on religion. Most interpretations of sectarian groups spring from the dominant functionalist perspectives and are afflicted by the same flaws.

One of the primary difficulties with current sociological approaches to the problem of differential sect affiliation is methodological. These approaches largely rely upon standard functional institutional analysis. In short, sect membership is seen as the outgrowth of social and psychological needs which small, exclusive religious groups are able to satisfy in modern industrial societies. These needs, in turn, are said to be created largely by the social structure. Owing to their lowly position in the class system, sect members are said to suffer from social discrimination and subordination and consequently, they are said to be searching for some sort of release from the frustration and humilia-

10. Ibid., p. 418. See also Paget Henry, "Durkheim's Sociology of Religion: A Critical Analysis." Cornell University, 1972.

tion produced by material and social deprivation. . . . The belief and worship of the sect act as a compensatory mechanism.[11]

Despite a reconsideration and modification of his earlier stance, Wilson continues to take the same basic line: "The individual, although no longer economically disinherited, may be one of the culturally neglected, and the sect may now compensate for this lack of cultural status and *savoir-faire*. Many members of the sect appear to suffer from a general inferiority feeling in regard to themselves and their religious organization; it reflects their awareness of educational, rather than economic deprivation."[12] Sectarian belief and affiliation are construed as a type of reaction formation to the problems of personal inferiority, in this case culturally rather than economically derived.

Although Schwartz professes reservations about the prevailing perspectives,[13] he utilizes them in his own research.

Social marginality and status deprivation sustain these sectarian forms of protest; these ideologies are precipitated by the strains associated with an untenable social status. More specifically, these ideologies serve as a means of formulating and dealing with status problems which are beyond immediate instrumental solutions. . . . [They] state status problems in terms which enable the actors to overcome, if in some cases only symbolically, obstacles to maintaining or increasing their self-respect which would otherwise appear insuperable to those with limited economic and social means.[14]

Schwartz's work is of particular value in that he confronts directly the issue of ideology or religious world view as one of the wellsprings of believer behavior. Much of the rest of the literature on sectarianism, however, is simply a particular case of the

11. Gary Schwartz, *Sect Ideologies and Social Status* (Chicago: University of Chicago Press, 1970), p. 76.

12. Wilson, *Sects and Society*, p. 321; cited in Schwartz, *Ideologies and Status*, p. 77.

13. "It is strange indeed when sociologists presumably concerned with religious organizations feel that their paramount task is not to account for their distinctively religious character." Schwartz, *Ideologies and Status*, p. 63.

14. Ibid., pp. 8, 53.

dominant functionalist perspectives at work in the sociology of religion that persistently "explain away" the phenomena in question.

The literature on Black religion presents similar problems, much of it again relying on functionalist orientations with the attendant limitations of vision.[15] The work on Black sectarian movements has identical difficulties. Here the observers have often allowed the distinctive practice of these groups to blind them to the underlying framework that informs their religion activity. Thus, in the 1920s Ira Reid attacked the smaller, less well-established churches in the following fashion:

Where one kind of church has progressed in the type of ministers selected and in the reformation of the church program, the other has become stuffed with cast-offs and religious criminals, who will not be denied. While the aggressive minority is pushing forward with intelligent and modern interpretation of a gospel that was once wholly emotionalized the satellites have glittered with their emotional paroxysms and illusive and illiterate mysticisms.[16]

Although Reid simply lumped the storefront churches and sects together and attacked them all as cults, later scholars have been more subtle in their critique. Thus Gunnar Myrdal in 1944 could invoke a functionalist analysis to argue that "If the church has been otherworldly in outlook and indulged in emotional ecstasy, it is primarily because the downtrodden common Negroes have craved religious escape from poverty and other tribulations." [17]

Arthur H. Fauset, also writing in the early 1940s, had the benefit of the functionalist vocabulary, which had been unavailable to Reid. Thus, Reid's harsh attack on the sectarian groups was displaced by a more dispassionate, "scientific" discourse. Fauset adds a positive note that is missing from Reid and earlier writers: "one is led to believe that, for many of their members, certain religious cults in northern communities, assist the transplanted southern worshipper, accustomed to the fixed racial mores and caste requirements of the South to adjust his psycho-

15. Frazier, "Analysis."
16. Reid, "Let Us Prey," p. 278.
17. Cited in Frazier, "Analysis," p. 155.

logical and emotional reactions to conditions in the North";[18] yet one still feels the impress of a functionalist framework in the spotlight on the accommodative and adjustive role of religious affiliation. The same interpretative schema persists in even more recent writers, albeit modified by more positive notes à la Fauset. Thus, G. Norman Eddy noted:

Throughout the United States, there must be thousands of these little churches. What is their appeal? Why do these people worship in uncomfortable buildings when the denominational churches have more than enough room for them? Undoubtedly the answers to these questions are complex, yet three factors seem to be of particular importance: These groups provide (1) a sense of status to the member, (2) assurance of spiritual healing, (3) opportunity for emotional expression.[19]

For Eddy as for Fauset these churches serve positive *functions*. Those functions, however, most likely do not correspond to those the members would identify. Eddy notes: "I asked two or three why they didn't attend an imposing church only a block from where they worshipped. One reply was 'Who would we be over there?' They gave other answers too—*many of them theological;* but I suspect that this was the real answer. Over at the other, larger church, they would have to compete with persons of considerably higher status." [20] Like a number of other writers, Eddy is too ready to discount the religious reasons offered by the believers and to seize upon reasons relating affiliation to social status. Further, he goes on to state:

Yet equally significant to these people is the emotional release provided by their church. So important is this factor that church attendance occupies practically all of their free time. . . . Emotionalism charges their testimony services and their singing as well as their sermons. In a typical store-front group, there are a few young people but the majority are middle-aged or older. When they come in, many of them look haggard and beaten. Somebody . . . will begin a song. The

18. Fauset, *Black Gods,* p. 81.
19. Eddy, "Store-Front Religion," p. 71.
20. Ibid.; emphasis added.

drums, tambourines, piano and the washboard . . . take up a musical accompaniment. Everybody sings and claps hands to the rhythm. A few stamp their feet. Vibrations from the music swell through the body. . . . A jubilant atmosphere charged with deep feeling becomes inspired by the rhythm. This joyous feeling is contagious. . . . It is apparent that all have derived some ecstatic release from this kind of worship. In it they discover an opportunity to lose their sense of frustration and failure in the everyday world. And these people, with this fervid cathartic experience, typify most transitory local groups.[21]

Though Eddy acknowledges the importance of the functions he has already enumerated—attaining social status, and so on—the factor given most prominence in his discussions is that signifying emotional release. Eddy's discussion is especially useful in this context for the way in which it articulates another theme that is a hallmark of this literature. As he says later on in discussing the House of Prayer for All People, "For these people, direct emotional expression is the essence of religion." [22] For him, then, *feeling* becomes the key to understanding their activity. The adoption of emotionalism as the key to interpretation installs a psychological framework, over and beyond the functionalist sociologism adumbrated earlier. Both of these perspectives are alien to the believers' realm of experience, and both substitute a sociological grammar for one(s) by which the believers would comprehend their action. This may be an appropriate methodological strategy for some research, but when applied to religious organizations it too often effectively discounts the framework of meaning relevant to the believers themselves, thereby also discounting the seriousness of their intention.[23] The result is that the be-

21. Ibid., pp. 73–74.
22. Ibid., p. 77.
23. "The Negro slave had to do something about the status in which he found himself. He, being human and not animal or even animalistic, needed some way to focus his existence into some kind of tolerable harmony. The lens for this need was the Christian religion. As Radin has indicated, it might have been any ideology, but Christianity was closest at hand. Therefore, the Christian Church became the way out of disintegration and its function was, in Kluckhohn's terms, adjustive for the individual." Frazier, "Analysis," pp. 145–46.

lievers, as encountered by the investigator, become obscured by the veil of social science discourse. The sociologizing of their behavior and the psychologizing of their motivation are a much more subtle mode of attack than the straightforward assault of Reid, but they are just as damaging in their consequences for our understanding. Analysis, rather than being an explication of social action and meaning, becomes an obfuscation and a further barrier to understanding.

More recently, there have been tentative steps away from the perspectives heretofore dominant. Melvin Williams's work on a Black congregation in Pittsburgh avoids the difficulties exemplified by Eddy and others.[24] As an anthropologist working in an urban setting, he is concerned with the subcultural community aspects of this group.[25] Its existence as a sacral community takes a secondary place.[26] He is quite successful in enumerating such things as networks, friendships, habits, inertia—all the ties that bind and operate to sustain the organization; but these impress more as "side bets," [27] subordinate to the central wager.[28] By not

24. Melvin D. Williams, *Community in a Black Pentecostal Church* (Pittsburgh: University of Pittsburgh Press, 1974).

25. "The networks of social interaction, the competition with other subgroups in the urban context, the political dynamics of Zion leadership, the viable competition of Zion's membership, the distinctive life style, the structured relationships to outside organizations, the personal satisfactions that members express, as well as Zion's historical process, its church organization, the nature of its membership, its range of church-sponsored activities, and symbolic expressions—all culminate in those premises upon which I conceptualize Zion as a little community." Ibid., p. 181.

26. "Thus love and fellowship are the dominant interactional ideologies in Zion, reinforced by the fear of hell, sin, death and various other supernatural sanctions." Ibid., p. 180.

27. "Notes on the Concept of Commitment," in Howard S. Becker, *Sociological Work* (Chicago: Aldine, 1970), pp. 261–74.

28. "But from my point of view the most important deficiency in the contemporary sociological theory of religious affiliation is that it tends to underestimate the significance of normative variations in sect ideologies. This is quite strange because, as I noted earlier, the sect is clearly identified by its distinctive beliefs and moral teachings, and schisms in sect movements usually take the form of ideological warfare. The sect

confronting the underlying framework of belief, Williams's analysis, in part, begs the essential question of *why* people find their sociality in church as opposed to some other, less rigorous form of voluntary association. History, habit, prior investments of time and energy are all useful though partial explanations and do not suffice to explain the fundamental fact of religious commitment. This is not to deny the importance of the communitarian aspect of church life—in fact, this is one of the focuses of the present study—but the emphasis on community, without corresponding attention to the religious basis of motivation undergirding it, alters significantly the reality we seek to explicate. Religious phenomena once reduced to functionalist or other postulates are no longer the entities observed. They become impoverished, and our own understanding is correspondingly weakened.

Arnor Davis takes direct aim at the negative assessments often attached to Pentecostal-Holiness groups, for example, that they are mainly the refuge of the poor and those defeated by life's struggle and oppression—

Some of these young people have assured me that they plan to use their time and talents for the Holiness church's programs. According to the Howard University Chaplain of Holiness students, their areas of study range from liberal arts, law, medicine, dentistry, social work, and pharmacy, to engineering and architecture. The Holiness background is a major factor in motivating and encouraging these young people to prepare themselves for life in the social situation which confronts them and their churches.[29]

—or that they are strictly otherworldly and apolitical, even antipolitical—

During the 1968 riots and the Poor People's Campaign, Bishop Kelsey used his weekly radio programs to urge people to donate food, cloth-

---

member's religious identity is also directly tied to its ideology; he places his chance for salvation in the hands of its diagnosis of the proper way to reach this goal." Schwartz, *Ideologies and Status,* pp. 75–76.

29. Arnor S. Davis, "The Pentecostal Movement in Black Christianity," *The Black Church* 2, no. 1 (1972): 83.

ing, housing and help in any way possible. He again used his influence to get his ministers and others in Washington to register and
vote.[30]

In 1964 Bishop Williams was elected Vice Chairman of the Demo-
cratic Central Committee for the District of Columbia and served
with honor and distinction. His work alone is proof that Holiness
Churches are not totally other worldly, but are concerned about both
this world and the world hereafter.[31]

—or that they are out of step with contemporary needs and of
limited appeal, and so on. Davis is, however, reporting on his
personal and professional experience. His apologia for the "sanctified churches" is a "voice from the other side" and plainly
partisan. Such efforts as his and Williams's do not yet constitute
a break from earlier modes of analysis but do offer clues to new
directions. Our own concern here is to extend the discussion of
such churches in two ways: by invoking other categories for
analysis, and by confronting directly the religious basis for their
behavior.

Mount Calvary Explained

In dealing with the Mount Calvary church, I have attempted to take seriously the world as the believer understands
it. In this endeavor, the work done in the sociology of religion
from the phenomenological tradition of sociology has been most
useful. The work of Berger and Luckmann and that of Berger
have been especially useful in guiding the formulation of a
framework for understanding the Mount Calvary Holy Church
experience.[32] Their work has enabled an approach to the ritual
life of the church as the basic activity of the believing community, as historically rooted and socially produced by the faithful,
and as the context within which and by means of which the

30. Ibid., p. 87.
31. Ibid., p. 82.
32. Berger and Luckmann, *Social Construction;* Peter Berger, *The Sacred Canopy* (New York: Doubleday, 1967).

transcending realities to which the believer adheres are made manifest.[33]

Men forget. They must therefore be reminded over and over again. Religious ritual has been a crucial instrument in this process of "reminding." Again and again, it "makes present" to those who participate in it the fundamental reality-definitions and their appropriate legitimations. The farther back one goes historically, the more does one find religious ideation ... embedded in ritual activity—to use more modern terms, Theology embedded in worship. ... The performances of the ritual are closely linked to the reiteration of the sacred formulas that "make present" once more the names and deeds of the gods.[34]

This is not to imply that Berger and Luckmann provide an adequate solution to the problem of the explanation of religion. In the final analysis, they also fall prey to a sociologism, namely, the reduction of religion to symbols of and legitimations for society (à la Durkheim).[35] Their framework of analysis, nonetheless, has proved most useful for the formulation that follows. Rather than ignoring the explanations of church members themselves concerning what they do in church and what it means to them, a phenomenologically informed approach has allowed me to follow their understanding of their own religious activity and to incorporate it theoretically, thus avoiding psychologizing or other reductionist explanations.[36] The analysis that follows focuses on ritual performance as the basic metaphor and also as the basic activity of religious life. The ritual is viewed as the embodiment in action of the beliefs of the faithful and, as such, ought to be understood in light of that belief; that is, it is the religious world view (*Weltanschauung*) that makes the religious ritual

33. "The implication of the rootage of religion in human activity is *not* that religion is always a dependent variable in the history of a society, but rather that it derives its objective and subjective reality from human beings, who produce and reproduce it in their ongoing lives." Berger, *Sacred Canopy*, p. 48.
34. Ibid., p. 40.
35. Berger and Luckmann, *Social Construction*, p. 128.
36. Berger, *Sacred Canopy*, pp. 55 ff.

meaningful and comprehensible. Furthermore, ritual is the setting within which the beliefs themselves become meaningful. Thus, a dialectic obtains between the ideal and material elements whereby each is meaningful in terms of the other; the ontological status of ritual and that of belief are to be understood together and not separately. Lest the dialectical point be seen in too relativistic a light, it is important to note that the ritual is also the setting whereby the Transcendent, the Almighty, Jahweh, the Spirit is made present in history. It is through ritual practice (in the normal course of affairs) that God and man are brought together in epiphanies (*epiphania*) and kairotic moments (*kairos*). It is this collection of moments that ritual embodies and whose sum is the "meaning" of the religious experiences of Mount Calvary members.

For the Mount Calvary church member, the ritual activities that consume so much of his time are not autotelic. Services have their own immediate and obvious purposes—to praise the Lord on Sunday, to raise money for the needs of some sponsoring auxiliary, and so on—but they also serve larger purposes. It is through the regular enactment of ritual that the church is "created." Church services provide a routinized framework for the ontological and religious verities around which members orient their lives. More specifically, they provide a context for confrontations between men and the Almighty and settings for manifestations of the presence of the Almighty within the ongoing lives of the participants. The presence of the Lord within the services is a manifestation of God in history, an epiphany. It is these ends of ritual that are of concern here.

As noted earlier, ritual performance is one of the key ways to define the church. Thus, one could argue that "Mt. Calvary people are those who perform this set of liturgical practices together." Of course, such a definition does not distinguish them from the number of other Pentecostal churches that practice basically the same rituals, but such a distinction is not needed here and the definition is adequate for the purpose. Ritual is indeed central, for if there were no common ritual life the church would not exist in conventional terms. Thus, it can also be argued that in at least two senses the exercise of ritual is also the creation of the church.[37] First, it is by means of ritual, "having church," that the group defines itself experientially. Second, ritual is the setting for religious symbols and beliefs that define the church and its members ideologically: "We understand our relation to God in this fashion, which is embodied in our service and legitimated by the presence of the Spirit in it." [38]

It is primarily in and through ritual performance that the church as social world is embodied and expressed. In the context of ritual, social relationships are defined and given substance. Deacons and ministers are seen as having a particular relationship to the group. All are brothers and sisters in Christ. Thus, the system of social relations that constitutes the church is modeled forth in its ritual. This is not to say that all relations are embodied in ritual, but the basic shape of such social relationships is adumbrated. Moreover, once embodied in ceremony, they persist in the ongoing lives of the members. Thus, the relationships that define people within the church persist outside the church as well. People continue to regard and address one another as Sister ————, Reverend ———— and Elder ————, even in the presence of non–church members. Moreover, the status relations they signify continue to guide interaction. Further, the church as embodied in its ritual life provides a model of the world in terms of the way

37. "To return once more to the dialectic between religious activity and religious ideation, there is a further aspect of this that is extremely important for the reality-maintaining task of religion. This aspect refers to the social structural prerequisites of any religious (or, for that matter, any other) reality-maintaining process. This may be formulated as follows: worlds are socially constructed and socially maintained. Their continuing reality, both objective ... and subjective ... depends upon *specific* social processes, namely those processes that ongoingly reconstruct and maintain the particular worlds in question. Conversely, the interruption of these social processes threatens the (objective and subjective) reality of the worlds in question." Ibid., p. 45.

38. "We can say that on the one hand, the institutional order is real only insofar as it is realized in performed roles and that, on the other hand, roles are representative of an institutional order that defines their character ... and from which they derive their objective sense." Berger and Luckmann, *Social Construction,* p. 79.

it "ought to be," in the sense that the church preaches a vision of the world in ideal terms and seeks to embody that ideal in its own life. Thus, the ever-present assumption that, "If only men would love God and live according to His law (as we do), the world would be fine." [39] Thus, we have the embodiment, or modeling forth, of the world on two levels: First, the social world of the church is defined and embodied in its rituals; second, the church's system of social relations is an image of the larger world as it "ought to be," which is one source of the missionary and evangelical impulse within Christianity generally and the Mount Calvary tradition in particular.

In Mount Calvary's case, however, the vision "of the world as church" is not the basis for active proselytization that it is among some of the newer Pentecostal and other religious groups that have emerged since the late 1960s. An accommodation exists between the church and the world, probably based on the southern theological tradition from which Mount Calvary comes. Though it exercised a prophetic evangelism toward the lives of individuals, this tradition stopped short of actively asserting such a posture vis-à-vis the society at large.[40] The result is that, whereas there is active proselytization of individuals for participation in the church and for conversion to Jesus Christ, the at-

39. The persistence of politics, economics, and other mundane problems of human society within the church itself is ignored at this point, the focus being on its ideal character. People, however, do note and condemn the persistence of "the marks of sin" within the church.

40. Liston Pope's treatment of the role of Gastonia churches during the Loray Mill strike in 1929 is instructive on this point. The churches were concerned about morality and justice, but only on a personal, individual level. The vast majority of them condemned both the strike and the Communists who led it. The strike and its leaders were attacking the social order to which the churches had accommodated themselves. This is the historical background against which one Boston pastor's comment is to be understood: "The church's role is to *help* the political sphere" (emphasis added). Hill (*Southern Churches*, p. 114) notes that "prior to the recently begun demise of the rural, folk-society, Southerners had no occasion to doubt that all that can and need be redeemed is individual persons, or to suppose that social conditions profoundly affect the welfare of the human spirit."

tempt to actualize the vision of the "world as church" is left implicit. Put another way, the church is concerned with the conversion of men as individuals; it does not admit the "stumbling block" of society and puts forth relatively little effort toward its conversion and salvation. Rather, the church "calls" individual men to salvation out of the wicked world. The salvation of which the church sees itself as guardian is a personal one to be worked out inside the church itself. The world is taken as a given and is sinful; thus, the call to salvation is a call to men to leave the world and enter the church. The call is directed not to the world (man in community or man in society), to work out a communal salvation but to men to work out their salvation as individuals within the church. It must be noted that these attitudes toward individual salvation and the world manifested by the Boston churches are a product not only of their history but also of their contemporary situation. The same ideological stance has led to somewhat different results in the southern situation. Among southern Blacks especially, the church occupied a central position in community life. For Blacks of rural background, as pointed out earlier, the church held a near monopoly in terms of extra-familial social life. Thus, the focus on individual salvation to the exclusion of "society" as a concern had less pietistic consequences because the church not only dominated but indeed constituted much of the social world of southern Blacks. Although not prophesying directly against society as such, the church, through its institutional hegemony, exercised immense control over the personal and moral lives of the people in the community.

Even in later years, as urbanization and rural depopulation altered the structure of southern social life, the church remained a major influence in these areas of people's lives, despite its loss of hegemony. The ideological and intellectual hegemony that it exercised over the lives of southern Blacks persisted for a period for those Black populations that migrated north, but the altered conditions of northern urban life limited the ideological and institutional dominance of the church in those times (1920s and 1930s) and does so today. The salvific concern for individuals to the exclusion of society characteristic of churches from that southern evangelical tradition led to their increasingly circumscribed societal impact in the North. They had been stripped of many of the extrareligious functions they had exercised in the South and, like many of their White coreligionists, they had never substantively addressed the larger questions of social justice and public morality. Consequently, increasing numbers of the population no longer assented to the church's ideological hegemony, and the influence of these churches became confined to their own congregations and to matters of faith and private morals. Thus, in the northern context, quietism is the result of transposing the church's southern heritage to the northern situation.[41] The modeling of the church experience in its ritual is important in that people develop (or reconfirm) a conception of Christians as "people who have a ritual life *together*" but also as people who do not share wider social or political concerns and who definitely do not act on such concerns in concert.[42]

The Service in Theoretical Perspective

Ritual is also important as the setting for the objectification of the church's religious symbols and beliefs. This is, of

41. Hill (*Southern Churches*, p. 113) notes that, "in 1965, the individualist approach promoted a skillfully organized campaign to rid Hot Springs, Arkansas of legalized gambling" at a time when little was being done about the issue of race. The point is that if the northern churches that share this southern heritage retained the ideological hegemony and popular support that the churches in the South have, they would have a more visible social impact. Their public posture would seem less quietistic—compare, for example, the impact of the Roman Catholic church in matters of public and sexual morality. Until very recently, Roman Catholicism had a very strong influence on public policy toward such issues as sex, pornography, and abortion, because of the ideological hegemony it exercised over the faithful and its willingness to express that hegemony in political terms (votes).

42. This is not to say that such social consciousness could not exist, only that it does not exist now and there is no indication that it will develop in the near future. There are individuals who have such concerns, but they do not integrate them into their understanding of faith.

course, a dialectical process. The symbols and beliefs provide the framework within which the intense ritual life is meaningful, and the rituals make real and give concrete social existence to these symbols and beliefs, which would otherwise exist only in the minds of men. We do not presume to address the question of the Almighty's existence here. Sociologists are guilty of sufficient hubris without our adding to that burden.

When people testify about the "goodness of the Lord" to them and witness to the effect of His moving in their lives, it is evidence for some that God indeed helps in men's affairs. When such a person tests his experience of the Lord's assistance in times of trouble and personal turmoil and testifies to the congregation about the "way that the Lord brought me through," he hears them vigorously affirm his testimony; this confirms his own experience and ties the dogma that "He makes a way out of no way" to his personal experience, that is, makes it meaningful in the religious framework. This is one of the key effects of testimony; when the individual testifies, not only does his experience of the Lord encourage and give edifying example to his fellows but their affirmation of this testimony sets the communal seal upon his experience. The congregation voices its agreement: "Yes, that was the Lord moving in your life."

More impressively, in prayer, when the one who is praying stands before the congregation, closes his eyes, and calls upon the Lord, the congregation does not doubt that he is truly communing with God. The prayer is not a static formula but an original communication between the person praying and the Almighty. The visible signs of effort in talking to the Lord—the closed eyes, the bowed or upturned head, the movement of the hands—demonstrate convincingly that the person is "pleading at the throne of Grace" for the intentions of the group in whose name he prays.[43]

43. A minister jokingly remarked that "some people have to impress you so much that they're holy that they speak in tongues when they say grace" and use such convincing evidence of being in touch with the "Spirit" on the slightest pretext. The irony is, of course, that they are not so holy as they would like to appear.

In the song service, there is a similar development. The hymns are traditional, the products of individual memories and the collective past, and they bear that weight; they are often religious doctrines set to music and are usually soul-stirring. The singing of such hymns in a communal setting strengthens communal bonds and feelings, infuses the doctrines with communal life, and can make people feel so good that they "shout for joy." [44] This ritual psalmody may even provide a vivid demonstration of the members' beliefs: "I was sinking deep in sin, / far from the peaceful shore, / sinking to rise no more. / Then the master of the sea, / heard my despairing cry, / from the waters lifted me, / how saved am I. / Love lifted me, Love lifted me." [45]

All of these facets come together in the sermon. The preacher utilizes Scripture and doctrine and discusses in real-life terms the power of God, "blessed assurance," the necessity of "living holy," or whatever theological subject he is attempting to illuminate. He makes use of gestures, mannerisms, and rhetorical devices to increase the forcefulness of his preaching.[46] Through his preaching, the medium of the messenger and the message, the Word is mediated to the congregation in vital and readily understandable terms. The Word is literally fleshed out and dwells as a real, substantial, and concrete entity in people's lives.[47] It gives

44. It also connects one to a history of singing these hymns and can recall to mind last week, last month, or several years ago when "Sister ———— witnessed for fifteen minutes behind that hymn."

45. Not infrequently, the feelings generated by the hymn singing literally "lift" people and force them to give vent to their joy. Shouting during the devotional service, however, is more likely to occur at revivals and special services than at the regular Sunday services.

46. There is a specific grammar and vocabulary of physical and verbal techniques, and each minister develops his own idiom. Commentators usually label this style of preaching as "highly emotional" and presume that the preachers become excited. They do become quite "worked up," but this is primarily due to the effort required to generate a good homiletic performance. It is usual for a moderately energetic preacher to be soaked with perspiration when he or she finishes.

47. The myths, symbols, and articles of faith of the congregation are given concrete form; they are embodied in concrete images. The people's faith is made real in this way; it is clothed in flesh. Thus, "for partici-

light to their lives immediately and often for long periods afterward.[48]

As noted in the previous section, the sermon is not an effort solely on the part of the preacher. The congregation actively participates in its "production." As in testimony, people lend their support and affirm his sentiments. Depending on the congregation, they may even stand and actively exhort him to "go 'head," "help yourself," "make it right," and so on. Thus, the fleshing out of the ideas and symbols of belief through the Word is truly a collective enterprise. In addition to being a vehicle for the reaching out of the Divine, the messenger also becomes the spokesman for the congregation, the "mouthpiece for the consensus" in the ritual moment. He speaks to and for the congregation, with their concurrence and participation. Indeed, there is often an interrelation between the congregation's participation and the success of the message in giving flesh and substance to the "mysteries of faith." When confronted by a dead congregation, a speaker may often find his own efforts faltering. Without the encouragement of the congregation, he may be unable to clothe his thoughts in original or soul-stirring imagery. As a result, his sermon may be "just words." Faced with this situation, a preacher will often enlist the congregation's help: "Won't

---

pants, their ritual performances are in addition enactments, materializations, realizations of it—not only models for the believing of it. In these plastic dramas, men attain their faith as they portray it." Clifford Geertz, "Religion as a Cultural System," in *Anthropological Approaches to the Study of Religions,* ed. Michael Banton (New York: Praeger, 1966), p. 29.

48. "I went to church one night, I felt like I was going under. I can't remember the Scripture, but the subject was 'Hope thou in God' and the question was 'Why art thou cast down, O my soul, and why are thou disquieted within me?' and 'Hope thou in God, for the Lord is the health of my countenance and my God.' And after the message, I felt so different, I felt lifted. I felt a reason for being and for living; for I was reminded that God loved me and cared for me. I left there a changed person." Quotation from interview with Beta member. It is noteworthy that the service referred to had occurred more than seven years previously. Her comment is not an unusual one.

you say 'Amen'?" ("Amen.") "Say 'Amen' again." ("Amen.")
Conversely, a congregation may give a preacher much encouragement, and he still may not be able to "get into it." The result
is the same. This effort is simply and clearly a collective one.

In addition to being the embodiment of symbols and dogma,
messages are designed for the purpose of making the "Spirit of
the Lord" real to the participants in the ritual. Ritual thus embodies faith in two ways: It embodies the articles of faith in real
terms, and, equally importantly, it makes the subject of that faith
("the Spirit of God Himself") real and present to the believer.
This often happens when the message builds to a high pitch that
is sustained for several minutes. The "Spirit" often takes hold of
the preacher; he gets "into gear," into "high G," abandons his
notes, and preaches "out of his heart," "out of his soul," "out of
the Spirit." "The man of God really preached out of the Spirit
tonight, didn't he?" "Amen, sure did." "Amen!" His preaching
becomes inspired, the sharpness and originality of his images and
metaphors increase, and the congregation keeps up its affirmation and encouragement. When all the elements are together, the
preacher is "making it right," and the congregation is right with
him, exhorting and encouraging, the dynamics and chemistry of
the situation lead to an epiphany, and the "Spirit of the Lord"
may become manifest in the church. Its presence is felt and may
in fact be seen by several people.[49] This manifestation of the
presence of the Lord is important and is a goal of this style of
preaching. Such an epiphany is "proof" of one's faith. When the
Lord is present to an individual, he knows that Jesus and the
faith to which he subscribes is real. A preacher who is unable to

49. Reference is often made to an event at Alpha church: The present
pastor of Beta church was preaching at Alpha church, and "the Spirit
go so high" that there was a heavy mist all through the church. Things
got so cloudy that one could hardly see. "I thought it was my eyes, so
I did like this [brushed hand across face and shook head], but it didn't
go away and then I looked and Sister ——— saw it too." On another
occasion when the pastor of Alpha church was preaching, "the anoint-
ing get on him so heavy that his whole countenance changed and ———
looked just like his father. ——— and Mother saw it too."

generate such epiphanies is not "successful" or popular.[50] There is, on the other hand, awareness on the part of ministers that the efficacy of their preaching lies not in how good it makes people feel, how much it makes them shout and carry on, but in the internal dispositions it creates or sustains in them.[51] The popular standard still demands "passion" in preaching, however, and generally rewards such preachers with large crowds and, equally important, large offerings.

Because of its evangelical origins, preaching is also specifically directed at the sinner. One goal of the message is to force a confrontation between the sinner and the Almighty; through the facets of his preaching—the vigor, the verbal and physical gimmickry, the power of his images—the messenger brings about a kairotic moment where the "Lord is made manifest" to the sinner, who must choose "aye or nay"—either acknowledge his sins before the church and the Almighty who has been made present to him through the message or reject the Lord and the salvation that is offered to him. The purpose of the altar call is to force that choice upon sinners. It is a central part of the church's theological heritage, and ministers recognize it as an important part of their ministry.[52] Sinners also recognize the po-

50. Another minister, not in Mount Calvary, with whom I discussed some of these issues noted that he had once preached a sermon that was not very vigorous. One of his parishioners angrily accused him of not having done his job. Because the minister had not "shouted and carried on," the parishioner had not "been spiritually transported" and felt shortchanged because the minister had given him less of an experience than he felt entitled to.

51. A Mount Calvary minister was preaching at a church not in Mount Calvary and told the congregation that the worth of a service was not in the ecstatic feelings engendered but in the internal dispositions it generated. Afterward, they told him that that was the first time they had heard the idea.

52. After some particularly inspired preaching at a revival, no one responded to the altar call. The ministers commented to the effect that if the sinner did not respond to such inspired preaching he would be reminded of his refusal on Judgment Day. Fear was expressed for the soul who did not heed the call. The preacher had discharged her duty after delivering such a powerful message. Her part had been done.

tency of such preaching and will avoid certain preachers to avoid the confrontation with God. They fear that when confronted they will have to choose to be saved, give up their "lives of sin," and "live holy."

It should be noted that there is a pervasive sense in the churches that there are vastly more "sinners" than "saints." Not only is this true in the sense that there are more people outside the church than inside; it is true in the more specific sense that there are many people who share the ideological universe mediated and symbolized by the church but who have withdrawn their assent to it. They accept its world view as real but violate its rules (which they accept as valid). These people are properly "sinners" because they "know" that Jesus died for their sins and that "they must confess their sins and acknowledge Him as their personal and in-dwelling savior," yet they choose not to do so.[53]

Thus, although these churches (the Mount Calvary Boston churches in particular and Pentecostal churches generally) are relatively small in membership, there is a large population that acknowledges the reality of the churches' vision but is "yet unsaved." As long as ritual continues to make real the articles of faith and to make present the Lord, this world will maintain its validity, at least for those who share its heritage.

After all the sociologizing and psychologizing have been accounted for, it can be seen that the key to unlocking the meaning of Mount Calvary is its liturgical life, not because its ritual practices are chants invoked to escape the "real-world" oppression of Karma's wheel, or magical formulas whose iteration will weave

53. The question is naturally asked: How is it that this church world view retains such a firmness in reality, even for those who are now outside it? The answer is twofold: First, southern Blacks especially grew up in a world where the church held ideological hegemony or at least dominance. Thus, this is the way life was understood; that is, they understood reality to be this way. Second, this church world view remains available to them because there are so many churches that still invoke this reality. Although it may no longer govern their lives, this world view is regularly brought to their attention. In this regard, see Berger, *Sacred Canopy,* chap. 2, "Religion and World Maintenance," esp. pp. 48–51.

a required spell over the believer and the proceedings, but because it is a celebration not just for the individual but for the community, too, of its life in faith. It is in liturgical action that the adherent confirms and reconfirms within the community his belief and experience of the power of God. This life in liturgy is important in other ways, too: as a sacral space by means of which the Lord is manifested to the faithful and as the *kairos* in which the sinner is brought to an encounter with the Almighty and offered the choice of salvation. The members spend significant amounts of time in ritual observance—one of the reasons that the church is often defined as "the worshiping community."

The character of this life has shifted over time. At the turn of the century, the fundamentalist evangelical tradition of which Pentecostalism (and thus Mount Calvary) was a variant was still the dominant world view in the South. It set the categories for life in general. There were plenty of "unsaved souls, sinners, and backsliders" then, too, but the hegemony of the ontology provided by the religious tradition was unthreatened.

This was no longer true in the North, for with the rise of a large-scale, urban, industrialized society Protestantism was fighting a rearguard action against an emergent consciousness defined in nonreligious categories. The root symbols and principles by which men lived were emancipated from ecclesiastical domination. The same economic dynamism, however, that fueled the breakup of the old ontological order brought to these same cities a growing population of Blacks who did not share the new secular freedom and, ironically, were still in sympathetic touch with a religiously grounded order that had been largely left behind in these cities. Furthermore, it was this migration that provided the soil for Holiness–Pentecostal expansion in the cities. This generation of Black folk is now passing, and their offspring seem to have been shaped more by the dominant categories of secular urban life than by the tradition of biblical literalism and the fundamentalism of the churches. This poses a basic challenge for these churches and for Mount Calvary in particular. It strikes right at the heart of church vitality. The decline of a population in touch with the church's world view forecasts declining fortunes for the worshiping community. People who do not share or who reject its experience of "the power of God" and "the infilling of the Holy Spirit" are not interested in sharing a liturgical performance that celebrates that knowledge in faith and (re)creates that experience in the here and now.

The Church as Social World

The performance of ritual, although crucial, is not the sole defining characteristic of the life of the church. As noted earlier, the church as social system is modeled forth in ritual, but there are facets of the social system not schematized in its ritual practice. In terms of its organization, Mount Calvary Holy Church has a well-defined national hierarchical structure. It is organized around a two-person executive—presiding and vice bishops—assisted by two national boards, a National Board of Bishops and a National Board of Presbytery. They in turn are assisted by a full complement of executive officers, including a national secretary, an assistant national secretary and corresponding secretary, a national and an assistant national mother, a national and an assistant national elder, a national and an assistant national business manager, and so on. There are also state structures, which are simpler copies of the national organization. Despite the church's formal structure, it seems to run in fact along less rigidly formalized lines. Ordinary members of the churches experience a local structure determined largely by the particular congregation.

A Background of Organization

Within local congregations, pastors are the major figures of authority. They exercise the bulk of the control within the congregation, no matter what are the formally prescribed lines of authority. They are supposed to be aided by "assistant pastors," yet only Gamma church currently has an assistant.[1] The rest of the congregational organization is subordinate to the pastor. Deacons generally assist the pastor and are often specifically charged with leading devotional services and taking up the offerings. They are also physically in charge of the church, keeping the keys and even cleaning it. Church mothers are generally older women and are assigned a specific "motherly" role: "Her duty is to help the pastor out, to support the programs, to keep the children straight, to keep the young women straight. There are so many things that a young woman would prefer to talk to a church mother about, rather than going to the pastor." In cases where the pastor is married, and men most often are, his wife is the "First Lady." This is partly an honorific, but she sometimes takes on aspects of the church-mother role, even though the two roles are formally separated because of the bond between the First Lady and the pastor. There are often "associated ministers," who are not assistant pastors but are rather ministers without churches of their own who join the church as members. They assist the pastor and are assigned to preach, take up offerings, and take charge of the pulpit. There are also "missionaries" and "evangelists," who are usually women; they are not ordained ministers, although they have a missionary "license" and legally receive ministers' benefits, such as reduced fares on railroads. They preach and are addressed as "Reverend" by the church. They are specifically charged with visiting the sick and doing missionary and evangelistic work, which is often a step toward full ordination.

1. At Alpha church, this is a function partly of size in that the current congregation is so small; also, there are no associated ministers who might fill this role. Because of the small size, several offices within the church remain unfilled, for example, pastor of the Junior Church, a young people's practicum for adult church roles. At Beta, the founder was pastor, and the current pastor was his assistant. She is now pastor and has named no assistant. There are, however, some twenty-odd "associated ministers" who are members there. Politics undoubtedly plays a role in one of them not being selected for this purpose.

Another important office in terms of congregational structure is that of secretary, and it is invariably held by a woman. Each local church is supposed to have someone in this position, which combines the functions of bookkeeper, treasurer, and secretary. The church secretary keeps accounts of all money received by the church and keeps minutes of church meetings and of church services.[2] The position is thus an important one and, depending on the person and on the pastor of the church, may have additional influence.

There are, in addition, a number of secondary church organizations within the individual congregations. The Sunday School, the Junior Church, the Pastor's Aid Society, and the Nurses' Guild are examples. Each sponsors a program of services. Some of the auxiliaries have regular functions in the church relating to services—for example, nurses and ushers both have specific roles within church services; all, however, have financial obligations to the church: "Each auxiliary is supposed to report to the Convocation with $150." Thus, each organization must raise that amount and send it as an assessment to the yearly Convocation. Auxiliaries sponsor services to build up their treasuries, and the association of ritual practice with money raising is partly responsible for the constant round of services and revivals.[3] For smaller congregations, this is a heavy burden, for the money so raised is actually turned over to the national body. If several auxiliaries "report" the prescribed amounts, the loss of revenue for the local church can be substantial.[4]

2. In Beta church, this extends to announcing the tithes of members at the end of the service.
3. Such services are often tied to monetary rationales: "We're going over there to show them how to give some money [*general chuckling*], so save your money. We want to give them a good offering." Sunday announcement.
4. This is one of the "costs" of membership in the Mount Calvary body, and it is undoubtedly a contributing factor when churches leave the body. This kind of local taxation, however, is apparently the main source of income for the national organization.

Each auxiliary has its own set of officers. In each Boston case, the pastor determines the presidents (and presumably the other officers) of the organizations. There is no recourse from the pastor's authority in practical fact. Before the founder's death, a member could take a grievance to him personally. Since then, however, the authority of the pastors has become almost impossible to challenge.[5] This centralization of authority in the pastor's hands leads inevitably to complaints on the part of members, although grievances are not generally publicly voiced.[6] Thus, within the Boston congregations, there is not the open factionalism on questions of power and control that characterizes other organizations (including churches). This is due in part to the self-image of the church as a "community of saints," but it is also a result of the small scale of the Boston churches and of the way in which pastoral authority functions at the level of personal relations.

An important area of complaint understandably involves church business. Each church is supposed to hold a quarterly business meeting,[7] where church business is discussed, financial reports are submitted, and future fiscal and official church policy is determined. Full reports of such meetings are kept by the secretaries. A clear illustration of the pastor's power is provided by these meetings. There is a general complaint in the churches regarding monetary matters; the members feel that too much money is being taken from them and that no adequate account

5. There is a mechanism for bringing grievances to the Convocation, but in terms of ongoing, everyday relations, the pastor has unassailable authority. If a pastor and a member disagree, the member must yield or leave the church.

6. Members often complain in private of the autocratic nature of authority and say that their talents are neither recognized nor utilized. This has large personal dimensions from which Beta church apparently suffers more than Alpha church.

7. "Every church shall have at least four sacramental meetings during the year, and at every quarterly meeting, there shall be a session, of conference of the church, for the transaction of business in which all the members in regular standing may participate." *Manual* of the Mount Calvary Holy Church, p. 8, para. 5.

of it is given.[8] These complaints are rarely heard at such meetings, however, nor is there full and open financial discussion, despite the public profession of "openness" about church business.[9] Members complain privately, but when presented in business meetings with the opportunity to voice their complaints and publicly ask pointed questions of church officials, most decline to do so. They are apparently intimidated by the situation and the officials.[10] As a result, pastors continue to control matters, and members grumble in silence.

Despite the crush of local church activity—the continuing round of local services and revivals, for example—there is an active sense of being part of the larger Mount Calvary body. This sense is communicated in several ways. The system of financial obligation to the national body is an important reminder of the bonds linking the churches. Auxiliaries periodically remember their fiscal responsibilities to the national body, and officers discuss how they are going to meet assessments to the yearly Convocation. Auxiliaries also send members to the yearly Convocation to provide representation from the local level in these national deliberations.[11] National officials often "come through"

8. People complained of the irregularity of business meetings; in Alpha church, there were fewer than the four specified in the *Manual*. There was no complaint that funds were being misappropriated. Rather, members complained that they were not informed of how money was being spent. Certain members were felt to have undue influence in such decisions, whereas others' opinions were rarely consulted.
9. None of the congregations submits a budget to the members for consideration, although the books are "open." In private discussion, complaints tended to be generalized and not pointed. When pressed, most members felt that they had little or no input as to how money was spent nor were they consulted in the making of major policy decisions.
10. When queried as to why they did not raise their objections when given the opportunity to do so at business meetings, members excused themselves, saying: "It wouldn't do any good," "The pastor would think I didn't trust him/her," "What could I do?" and so on.
11. There are separate national conventions for ushers, Junior Church, et al., and there are a number of other national meetings including a biannual "Council meeting." The Sunday School, the Young People's Holiness Association (YPHA), and the missionaries have separate days of recognition at both state and national convocations.

to preach revivals and visit the local churches. This regular visitation is important in maintaining ties. Until his death, the founder constantly traveled about, visiting his churches. The personal loyalty maintained by this itinerary was an important factor in keeping the national body together. His successor has continued the pattern.

The National Convocation of the church is the prime collective expression of this larger unity. Members, ministers, and officials from Mount Calvary churches around the country gather for a week of service, fellowship, and the conduct of church business. Ties of friendship and association are created and revived, and the national church assumes an actual social existence. Because this gathering is always held in Boston, and because the national headquarters is located in Boston, the consciousness of a national identity is perhaps stronger in the Boston churches than elsewhere.[12] National officials are spread throughout the country in terms of residence, however, and this factor together with regularly scheduled visits helps to strengthen the national consciousness among the other churches.

Because of the costs and difficulties involved (transportation and living expenses, time off from work, family obligations, and so on), relatively few people actually attend the national meetings, especially those not held in their own towns. For most people, therefore, their primary experiences of the church as other than a local organization are the intercongregational fellowship and state meetings that tie the congregations together on a statewide, regional basis. The Boston churches are the only ones in Massachusetts; thus, they make up a state convocation of their own. New York has churches both in the New York City metropolitan area and across New York State, and regular fellowship plays a lesser role there because of the distances between churches. Some 500 miles separate the Buffalo and New York City congregations, for example.

As noted before, the Boston churches try to coordinate their

12. Thus, the founder and his successor were frequently in Boston on church business.

programs to a certain extent, supporting each other's revivals and special services. Further, there is a general habit of fellowship between the churches so that intervisitation is a regular occurrence with or without revivals as a rationale.[13] "I would have service at eleven o'clock on time. We'd get out at half past twelve, quarter to one, done our little shouting, and cut out. We had a chance to go down to ——— church. They wouldn't get out till two, three o'clock. Even during the week, we'd go to their services." In addition to this informal fellowship, there are more structured relations. One congregation may invite one or both of the others for a "special service" of an auxiliary or may ask an associated minister from another congregation to preach; he in turn may bring along some members from his own congregation. One pastor may be invited to preach a revival at one of the other churches or to participate in another congregation's anniversary (for the church's and pastor's anniversaries, it is the usual practice to have a week of services precede these events and to invite a different church and speaker each night). Finally, there are state meetings and organizations that tie the Boston churches into a larger structure. Just as there is a National Convocation, each state has its own convocation, a smaller version of the national meeting. These state meetings are in a sense more important for the Boston churches than the National Convocation because these are completely their own, although national figures do appear. In addition, state officers of the various organizations sometimes live out of state and return for the convocation.[14] The pattern of the state meetings parallels that of the National Convocation, although on a much smaller scale.

13. Because the pastor of Alpha church is also the "bishop and state overseer," he regularly visits the other two churches. It is not unusual for members of one congregation to "visit" another congregation for service; groups from one congregation will often visit another congregation's service if it is still going on when theirs is finished.

14. Of the state officials in 1972, three were not living in Massachusetts: the president of the YPHA, the state superintendent of the Sunday School, and the state secretary. Although this practice was tolerated by the founder, his successor has given indications of eliminating it.

This is the organizational context within which a Mount Calvary identity is established; it is bounded primarily by the limits
of the congregation and its liturgical life but includes elements
of a national group consciousness (for example, "We in Mount
Calvary . . ."). In the Boston case, the larger group consciousness is heightened by Boston's position as national headquarters
of the church and by the convenient metropolitan location of the
state's churches.

The Family of Mount Calvary

Familial interconnections are another important social
factor; they affect both the identity and the structural strength of
the church on all three levels—local, regional, and national. This
factor is important in the Mount Calvary national body to varying degrees, but in Boston its significance usually goes unattended.
Four of the twelve current members of the Alpha church are
members of the pastor's family, and several other church members have familial ties. Prior to 1971, when the membership was
much larger, family ties were also important in maintaining the
church; the loss of two or three families reduced the church's
size by more than one half. In the Beta church, family ties are
not so important, partly because of the predominance in the congregation of women whose husbands are either nonmembers or
absent from the home and whose children reject the church upon
reaching adolescence. There are several mother–daughter combinations within the church, however, and mothers with young
children bring them to church. In addition, there are familial
links among the three churches; for example, a member of one
congregation may have a sibling or other relative in another congregation. These familial bonds within the church serve as an
additional bond of allegiance and deepen a member's involvement in the web of affiliation.[15]

15. For an analytical discussion of these bonds, see "Elements of Identification with an Occupation," in Becker, *Sociological Work*, pp. 177 ff.
Becker also discusses the notion of "side bets" (p. 266) as added constraints on a person to maintain proper behavior and "face." He sub-

Family ties are important on another level within the Mount Calvary churches. There is a rhetoric of familial relations that is used within the church to describe ties between different people. Thus, the founder was universally referred to as "Dad" and was so regarded by many in the church. For those who served on the evangelistic teams, especially, the founder was often a surrogate parent. A number of members who joined the church through him related to him as to a father. He in turn dealt with both evangelistic team members and regular members as his sons and daughters, his children. The current pastor of Beta church is addressed as "Mama ———," the current senior bishop as "Daddy ———"; regular members address one another as "Brother" and "Sister." [16] This mimicking of familial and filial relations within the church is genuine within its limits, but association is limited to the church; there is not the comity among members outside the church that exists within. The pattern seems to be that members establish close familiarity with each other as members of the church but are not intimate much beyond that.[17]

These organizational factors are corollaries of the church's ritual life. The central dynamics of the church's life are outlined in its ritual practice, but there is also a background of social relations and organization not schematized in the church's liturgical life. These relations include state and national convocations and council meetings, which are manifestations of the state and national life of the church; church auxiliaries and their state and national meetings; and local events, business meetings, and the

---

sumes under "side bets" generalized cultural expectations, for example, good opinions of neighbors, personal ties that develop within the organization and are dependent on continuing organizational identity and affiliation, and so on. Cf. also Williams, *Community,* Introduction.

16. A succession of people described their church relationship in familial and filial terms. A former evangelistic team member noted: "We would go in and maybe be there a couple days or so, and Dad would tell us, 'Children, get ready, we'll leave out in the morning.'"

17. "Our paths very seldom cross except for the young ones who I see now and then. We're all in contact but don't visit each other's homes at all or have close friends."

web of financial obligations that knit the local churches, their auxiliaries, and the state and national church together. The numerous state and national events serve to maintain a sense of national identity within the church, a consciousness that is fostered by the continuous traveling of national officials.

In addition to these organizational and structural correlates of church identity and consciousness, more specific social and local group factors are important in maintaining commitment and involvement. Close and amicable relations between local churches are maintained and expressed by regular structured and impromptu intervisitation. There are a number of kinship bonds among members of the Mount Calvary churches, and a surrogate familiality further informs relationships within the church on a broader scale. The founder was a "father" for many church members, and the rhetoric of familial relations as well as the close bonds that often obtain in large, close-knit families are observed within the church, both locally and nationally.

These organizational and social factors serve to tie the church member into a complex web of affiliation and involvement and bind him or her more closely to the church. These added bonds of the church as social world serve to intensify the commitment of the believer and reinforce the primary relations and beliefs embodied in the church's ritual life.

The Church in the Social World

The Church as Institution

THE INSTITUTIONAL EXCEPTION. A distinctive feature of the Boston Mount Calvary churches, one that sets them apart from other Boston Pentecostal churches, is the way they have extended, albeit in their own small way, the vision of the church *as* world beyond the four walls of the church. The Mount Calvary church nationally has acquired property throughout the country and has established an orphanage and a home for unwed mothers in the South as well as a number of "conference homes" for the convenience of national officials and other visitors.[1] Two conference homes are located in Boston, one of which is used as the office of the national headquarters as well as operating as a quasireligious community. It is the home of the pastor and two other associated ministers of the Beta church. None of these people is married, and they are consequently almost completely dedicated to the church. Thus, a strong religious aura is attached to this household, strengthened by the fact that the founder made the house his headquarters and residence when he was in Boston and was the head of the household. This group has been able to

1. No list of church property holdings was available. A reliable informant reported that "people all over the country gave 'Dad' property which he gave to the church." There was some indication that church holdings were not insubstantial. The church holds title to at least five houses in Boston alone, in addition to the three churches. Little income was realized from these properties, however.

extend outside its walls the relationships and assumptions that govern life within the church, and they are thus able to live their day-to-day lives according to this vision.[2] This case may be unique, as there is another conference home in regular use in Boston that operates differently.[3] Not all of its occupants are members of Mount Calvary; nor are they all "saved"; consequently that house does not operate as a community. This house is much more "of the world," and the Mount Calvary members who live there cannot define the situation as "the world as church"; instead, they live as "Christians in the world." This is, moreover, an appropriate rubric for understanding the place of this church and its members within the wider society.

THE INSTITUTIONAL NORM. Despite the great amount of time spent in church and its importance in their lives, church members reside nonetheless in the larger world outside the church. Despite the nascent millenarianism ("And I ask you all to pray that I be the daughter that He is looking for in these last and evil days"), members must still go about their workaday lives. Thus, the question remains: How do these individual believers relate to the "world outside the walls," and further, how does the church as institution relate to that world (and the corollary, how does that world relate to the church)? It is with these questions that this section is concerned.

It appeared initially that Mount Calvary, that is, the organized, religious activity and the collectivity performing it, was the basis

2. This is so at least in theory. On an intimate, day-to-day basis, it is obviously more difficult to reproduce the vision of "the community of saints" as social fact. Church members are, after all, human and their interrelationships bear witness to that fact. The fact that two of the residents were members of evangelistic teams and that a third has been totally dedicated to the church for more than thirty years also contributes to the cohesion of the household.

3. The author knows of no other similar protoreligious communities within the church nationally, although their existence is possible. There are families within the church that approximate this religious vision, but it seems unlikely that there are other households like this Boston "conference home."

of a broader communal association.[4] The small size of the congregations, their regular intervisitation and apparent closeness,
and the rhetoric of filial and familial relations that was displayed
all suggested this. More particularly, it was thought that the
church fellowship provided an initial vehicle for wider extrareligious communality. It was presumed that people would form
close friendships based upon church affiliation, that church
groups would provide dating, courtship, and marriage partners,
and that young people would form peer groups on this basis also.
Observation has not confirmed this to be the case. It is true that
some friendships are formed through the church, and there have
been a few weddings performed over the last two years.[5] There
is also, as one would expect, some telephone contact. The over-
whelming majority of people queried, however, said that they
did not socialize with fellow members outside the church. There
are several apparent reasons for this: (1) Most adults work and
have family obligations; (2) few people live within walking distance of one another, and thus visiting is a larger proposition
than "going next door" or "up the street a-ways" (women especially feel that the streets are unsafe at night; (3) actual church
attendance requires much of the members' time (although week-
night attendance is fractional compared with that of Sunday).
This qualification is most applicable to Beta church, which has
the largest membership but also the largest proportion who attend church only on Sunday. The other two churches, being
smaller, exert more personal social pressure to attend and support the church. In addition, the following rationale was repeatedly offered:

I used to [socialize] but not now, because it was nice being with the
saints, but everybody takes things wrong. I don't have many men

4. This analysis applies mainly to "active" church members who attend
services during the week as well as on Sunday and who steadily participate in and support other aspects of church life. It is less applicable to
"cultural Christians" who attend church only on Sunday and who are
less committed to "holiness" as a way of life.
5. The pastor of Beta church reported four weddings at her church during this period; there were none at either of the other two churches.

friends. . . . I used to have men friends when I first come in. I had men preachers, but they go to cussing and swearing, and I don't like that even out in the world, and after you hear it all week long from work you don't want to hear it when you get with your friends. You think you got somebody to talk to about the Lord . . . and here they be cussing and swearing. . . . So I say, it's better to be by yourself. And if you go to a woman saint's house, they declare you goin' with them. So to keep it down, I stay away from them. . . . You can't do it here. . . . You go your way and I'll go my way.

Even among young people, the majority do not use the church as the basis of their comity, utilizing instead school and neighborhood for this purpose: "Most of the people in the church are just not my speed, so I just don't hang out with them." It should be clear, however, that the church is not simply a secondary association. For some, it may approach this,[6] but for the vast majority, rather than being the basis for broader communal association, Mount Calvary *is* that communal association. Insofar as most active members have a larger communal life outside their families, the church supplies it. For some, the church may be the only association to which they belong.[7] For all serious members, it is the main one.

But I wanted to be in Mount Calvary because I wanted to be in the church, because this is the only church and God is the only way that I can survive until He comes again. . . . The reason I'm in the church is that I love the things of the church. And I'm not only *in* the church, I'm *of* the church. Anybody can go to church and say "I'm in the church. I belong to the church." But I'm of the church, I'm a part of the church. I'm not going to just be playing or fooling around, but

6. There are a number of "Sunday-only" members of Beta church for whom this may be true, although their patterns of participation outside the church setting probably differ little from that of church "activists." They would regard Mount Calvary as more than a voluntary group because they retain their belief in its world view. Although they are free to alter their institutional affiliation, if they were simply "cultural Christians" it is unlikely that they would have joined a "sanctified" church.

7. This is to be expected because rates of organizational participation in the lower classes are low.

this ain't no plaything. And this is what I'd like to make my life out of.

Thus, although some with school-age children attend PTA meetings and others engage in work-related activities (credit unions or labor unions, for example; none known to the author is involved in organized sports activities such as bowling leagues), these involvements are secondary and for church members are voluntary associations, properly so-called. The church is an end in itself (although, technically, it is only an instrumentality to help "saints" get to the "Kingdom"). It is the temporal signification of the Truth.

The picture of Mount Calvary members that emerges at this level is of a population that participates in the world but does not "live" there. People work, eat and sleep, go to school, shop, vote, but their worldly lives are of secondary importance to them. Young people do not "party." Nor do adults socialize in this fashion (the prohibition of alcohol is involved here; people at parties drink liquor, and there may be pressure on a "saved" person to "follow the crowd"). Further, those who are "saved, sanctified, and Holy Ghost–filled" are supposed to "live holy," and this requires behaving differently from worldly people. If one went to parties like worldly people and did the things they do, there would be no perceptible difference between a person who claimed to be "saved" and one who was not.

Recreational activity is limited to movies, restaurants, family and church outings on holidays, television, and occasional Gospel or other church programs. This recreational pattern for adults is partly a function of their work lives; they simply do not have the leisure time, nor, being of the lower-middle and lower class, have they acquired the taste for books, concerts, and politics that characterizes some middle-class sectors of the wider population. Their church lives and the rigorous moral standards associated with Pentecostal practice serve to further circumscribe the amount of leisure and the kinds of recreation available to them.

It must be emphasized, however, that these individual members do participate in the world. They have to work, and their occupations range from working class to middle class, with some individual entrepreneurs among them.[8] There are few housewives in the Boston congregations; most women work either because they are single or single parents and have to support themselves and their children or because their added income is needed to meet the high cost of living. A number of adults participate in continuing or adult education programs, and there is a growing tendency among them to take advantage of newly available higher-education opportunities.[9]

The vast majority vote, and many have participated in one community organization or another.[10]

They had a meeting up here on the avenue for the new development of Roxbury. I used to attend quite a bit. But I don't go out too much on account of there is so much going on in the streets. I stopped going to it because a lot of the things they say they just say they are going to do. Three years I was going around there to meetings with them, and they never got around to doing anything. But they have a whole lot to say. I didn't see where my going was doing anything.

A lack of enthusiasm for community and poverty program politics is widespread and may be as much an indicator of the usefulness and viability of such programs and organizations as of the quietist attitudes of these church members.

Their association with their fellows on the job is, however, affected by their church status. Their peers are aware of their church affiliation (Black Pentecostal churches are held in low esteem by Blacks in higher-status churches as well as by those

8. At least three members of the Beta congregation have fair-sized businesses: a local bakery, a small supermarket, and a beauty supply business.

9. A Beta member currently works as a Black student counselor at a local state college and has made information about educational opportunities available to church members. Awareness of such opportunity is "in the air," and people repeatedly sought the author's advice as to whether and how they should continue their education.

10. Sixteen of nineteen persons queried on this question voted, and with two or three exceptions, in *both* of the last two elections; thirteen of the nineteen were involved in some community organization.

who are "unchurched"), and church members are often derided for their faith. On the other hand, Mount Calvary and other Pentecostal believers are not shy about their beliefs. "At my job they used to tell me that when I get to talking about Christ and them being saved and where they're going to spend eternity, they say I'm getting on a soap box. They always got a gag to throw at you. I don't try to push nothing down, but a lot of times they just want to see what you're going to say." Aside from the openness with which they acknowledge their rigorous faith and the critical attention it often brings, there seems little to visibly distinguish Mount Calvary members from their peers in their day-to-day lives outside the church context. They have no special occupations, no dietary restrictions, and no special relations with the state. Except for their churchgoing and the particular moral and leisure-time consequences associated with that, they appear similar to others of their socioeconomic status.

INTRAINSTITUTIONAL DIFFERENTIATION. Within this broad uniformity, there is differentiation as well as deviance within the congregations. The deviance is both major and minor, which is to be expected, for the relevant literature has shown deviance to be endemic, and Mount Calvary is no exception to this rule. Members have transgressed the full range of church and societal proscriptions—gambling, sex offenses, robbery, and so on. There have also been any number of minor transgressions. The point is not, however, to catalog the faults or instances of backsliding by church members but to note that, within the broad picture of uniformity, there are people who are different, not simply in their deviance from the standards of righteousness but in terms of their attitudes toward the world; that is, they differ substantially from the prevailing wisdom regarding things secular. They do not constitute a subgroup but are rather individuals within the church, where the lack of extraecclesiastical association contributes to their isolation. Other deviants are of a different order. Some are heterodox in one or another area of doctrine, a consequence of having at one time or another been members of different churches. Others differ from their fellows mainly in that they have an active interest in civic and political concerns; they are involved in various organizations and community groups and lack the signs of disenchantment that mark so many others within the church.

I'm on the Board of Directors of the Higher Education Program and Model Cities Agency. I'm working on Black Caucus [a forum for local Black politicians]. I'm head of Student Government. I'm part of the Evangelistic Association. I graduated from the United Fund Community Service School. This is to deal with the community at large in matters of health, education, and welfare. . . . The world opened up my eyes to my faith; as long as I was behind those four walls I was dead. . . . Mount Calvary snubs those who are worldly . . . but we have to get out among these people.[11]

Moreover, their "worldly" concern does not diminish their active involvement in the life of the church. Several are ministers or have "missionary licenses." Others are officers in the various auxiliaries, sing in the choir, and so on. In addition, they are as committed to the church as those with fewer civic concerns. "Mount Calvary is Mount Calvary like my arm is my arm. When Bishop Johnson was alive, he would come and fix everything, and Reverend ———— always tells the truth, and when Bishop ———— comes through he definitely puts everything together." They do tend to be more critical of the way things are managed: "I'll say I'm not happy at ———— [congregation], but I don't go church jumping either. The church is relevant and we need the church. I just like to walk into the church. The church is God's house." These individuals also differ somewhat from their fellows along ethical lines. They are not as traditionally orthodox in their belief and practice as the church as a whole professes to be: "I came to realize from observation, prayer, and becoming closer to God that there may be reasons where a person must drink for health, and that didn't mean you weren't saved." [12]

11. Six of twenty-five persons interviewed fall into this category. This is probably a higher percentage than in the general church population.

12. This sentiment was expressed to one degree or another by several members at both Alpha and Beta churches. Discontent is a greater problem for the Beta church, due mainly to personal components and not to any systemic factors.

Nor do they condemn smoking or partygoing as readily. These "liberal" deviations from traditional norms also crop up among more conventional members of the congregation, so the more politically concerned members have no monopoly on "liberal" ethics. At any rate, such formal proscriptions appear to be weakening generally within the Pentecostal tradition. At one time, no personal adornment was permitted—no jewelry, makeup, neckties—and some churches even discouraged children from playing games. These strictures have been gradually relaxed so that makeup, jewelry, and wigs are worn. The prohibition against gambling is still strong, although some buy state lottery tickets; others see nothing wrong with cardplaying as long as there is no "playing for money." This erosion of traditional strictures will no doubt continue.

The differentiation among members along lines of civic and political awareness and activity is of greater significance than may be apparent. It points to a divergence that might be described as "traditionalists" versus "modernists." The "traditionalists" have little or no external activity or concern and limit their sense of what is important in life to the church. The "modernists," although they are as active within the church as the traditionalists and adhere basically to the same practices and ideological forms, regard the "world" as an important sphere of concern and activity. Modernity, in the sense of a more liberal approach to church standards, extends beyond those with active civic concerns to include others who are simply less rigorous about the special moral strictures attached to the Pentecostal tradition (no drinking, smoking, gambling, and so on), because both sets of people share a less than complete acceptance of the traditional religious world view as conventionally applied to ethics and civic or secular involvement.[13] "The church founded by Dad is not what we have today. We need programs for children and

13. People were guarded about admitting deviance and political heterodoxy, and unless they were convinced of the interviewer's empathy, maintained the appearance of saintly perfection. Several refused to be taped and/or spoke in parables about the church and their real feelings in an effort to protect themselves from being quoted.

adults. We shouldn't be contained only right here. We have to be on the street. . . . This is one of the biggest downfalls. It's shutting the world out of the church. I'm a Holiness and an evangelist; I want to draw all people to Christ. Mount Calvary is secluded. It's ethnocentric in its beliefs." [14] Those with active civic concerns, especially, understand their faith as extending beyond concern with strictures and adherence to the bounds of Pentecostal tradition. They seek an added dimension to their faith or at least a deeper life within it. Their position is thus theologically and behaviorally more "modern."

Traditionalist and *modernist* are not rigid categories but are rather useful devices for giving form to otherwise unacknowledged differences within these congregations and for grouping people according to the strictness of their adherence to traditional belief and practice. Divergence from orthodoxy is generally manifested in regard to political activity and civic concerns; that is, it is related to personal and institutional practice regarding the interrelations between the church and civil society. At times it is manifested simply in terms of church strictures; some practices and beliefs are rejected as unnecessarily restrictive and/or untrue. The two manifestations usually, however, go hand in hand.

Modernity is not a "position" within the Boston churches. Modernists like other deviants remain isolated, "in the closet," so to speak. The traditional world view retains a publicly unchallenged hegemony, and traditionalists continue to assume that their "vision" fits the world. It is possible that this situation will change within the church. The simple development of modernists coming out of the closet would pose a serious challenge to the traditional world view and its exponents. Given the conditions of near-absolute pastoral authority, however, this is unlikely to happen in the Boston churches in the foreseeable future. On the other hand, an external threat to the church itself might

14. There is a problem of precision here, because that world view is not codified or rigid but "flexes" according to which church and which minister is expounding upon it. This "flex" is one source of new ideas. Thus, some ministers are more open to "worldly concerns" than others.

challenge the traditional view. In the only observed instance, however (see the section on practical politics, below), this did not occur. What is more likely to happen is that the modernists will either continue their deviance in silence or leave the church and find a more congenial one. In Boston, the former possibility seems more likely.

INSTITUTIONAL PARTICULARITIES. The preeminence of the traditional world view among the membership is indicative of the position of the Mount Calvary churches within the larger Black community. The Alpha church is in a low-income area adjacent to several low-income housing projects. The church has never made a substantial impact on the life of the area. Although its membership is working class, it has had no relationship with the projects' inhabitants who, because of proximity, form a large body of prospective members. Until recently, only a few of its members lived within walking distance; the church was mainly a "commuter" or "downtown" church.[15] The previous pastor attempted to draw project dwellers into the church.

didn't none of them join but they would come in. Most I had was young people, and they would come in because I had young people, and they would come in maybe Sunday morning and then I wouldn't see them any more. . . . I asked them, "Why don't you come in and join the church?" They said, "Well, I belong here, or I go up there." Some of them belonged to another little church down there, the Church of God, near where Daddy Grace's church was. They'd say, "I like your service, I like the way you carry it out." "Well, why don't you join?" "Well, I'm not ready."

Despite the Pentecostal concern for evangelism, the current pastor has not sought out this population, and this is a factor in the small size of his congregation. Although "converting the lost" is an often-voiced concern, an effective outreach program has been lacking in this church. Further, an ongoing sociopolitical

15. Recently another low-income project was completed, and two of the members and their families moved into it, thus shifting the balance between those within walking distance and those who must drive or use public transportation.

concern has not been a part of this church's approach. The same appears to be true of the Gamma church. It remains a small congregation with a "commuter" membership. It has a negligible impact on its neighborhood and evinces primarily a religious concern. There are special considerations in this case, however (see chapter 3).

The Beta church is in a somewhat different position relative to the community in which it exists. It has a lower-middle-class character, although there are both middle-middle and lower-class members as well as several known to the author who could be classed as petit bourgeois.[16] It has more members who live fairly close to the church than do the other two churches, and it has had some involvement in the social and political life of the community, although not a substantial amount. It also has a much bigger plant to make available for community use and has sponsored occasional dinners for senior citizens in the area (the founder had a special concern for the elderly, and the impetus for these dinners came from his concern). It has tentative plans for a day-care center in the church. The current pastor has served on the local Model Cities board as well as in other civic organizations. She does not, however, have a regular salaried occupation other than the church and thus has more time to devote to "public life" than the pastor at Alpha church or those of the other small Pentecostal churches in the community.

Relations to Secular Politics

It should be clear from the earlier discussion that some social and political concerns are evident within these congregations. Such concerns, however, are not at the corporate or institutional level but remain primarily personal. Moreover, this appears to be true for Boston's Black churches as a group. The negligible influence of these churches on community life is usually interpreted as a result of the apolitical or reactionary political

16. Cf. chap. 2, above, for a fuller description of this church and its community setting; see also p. 122, n. 8.

position of Pentecostal religion. This interpretation is flawed by the implicit assumption that politics or political action is the focus of these churches' concern. More accurately, questions regarding the political stance of these churches—in this case, the Boston Mount Calvary churches—must be phrased in terms that take into account the framework within which these churches understand themselves. They see their purpose as "the saving of souls." The individualism and latent millenarianism of the tradition from which the Mount Calvary churches come further remove consideration of society, that is, secular society, from the churches' purview, for these factors reinforce the tendency to understand the world solely in terms of the goal of individual salvation. We have seen how this same theological tradition has led to less significant pietistic consequences in the southern context. The question is, therefore: What social role do Boston's Mount Calvary churches play within their present situation, that is, within a minority community that is increasingly agitated about its inequitable position within the larger society?

The answer is simply that they do not understand themselves corporately as having a political role. They do not see themselves as institutions engaged in struggle on a secular front for social, political, and economic goods for an oppressed community. Insofar as the "struggle" is perceived, individuals respond on a personal level, whereas the church's response is to "call all men to Christ."

So God has a case history on us. He has a case history on us from Adam on up to the present time. This is what one of God's diagnoses about us was—it's also in the Psalms; Paul quotes it, I believe, in Romans. Paul says that God looked down from heaven among the children of men, to see if there were any that did good or understood. God wasn't looking for those that were doing evil; He saw all of that. But He was searching for one who was doing good. And the word of God says—after God with His X-ray eye, with all His wisdom and knowledge—it says His eyes go to and from throughout the whole world, beholding the good and the evil, and His diagnosis was, and His verdict was, *"No, there is no, not one."* God said he couldn't find one that did good, and then Paul in Romans begins to name off what

God saw in us. He said, "They have become altogether filthy, in their mouths is the poison of asps; they are deceitful and their feet are swift to hunt or shed blood; misery and destruction are in their way, and the way of peace they have not known." My Lord, this is God's diagnosis of our case. Sad case, isn't it? We bad off sick.... Sick, Jesus said: "He that is well needeth no physician," but he that is sick, if you'd only acknowledge that you're sick, that you're a sinner, that you need Christ, that you need the physician.... You need Christ.... He's the master of physicians.

This is not the only statement that Mount Calvary preachers make about the world and its problems, but it is representative, both of them and of the tradition from which they come. Individual preachers occasionally voice other sentiments, for instance this one from a Sunday School class: "*Q*. In a case like that [a theft with social policy implications], who is to blame for it? *A*. Those who have the power to change it. It doesn't excuse the individual who does it, but the responsibility is with those who have the power and wealth to change it." On another occasion a minister remarked during a discussion, "The earth could produce and feed everyone that God allowed to come [be born], if men would not put up fences and talk about things as mine." A more cogent topical response was heard after the American terror bombing of North Vietnam in December 1972, when the president's advisor, Henry Kissinger, declared that "peace is at hand." One pastor announced from the pulpit the following Sunday, "We don't care who does it, whether king, president, Nixon, whoever; it's wrong and we condemn it. It is evil in the sight of God. Here we are in the season of peace and he's dropping bombs, killing everything that moves. But Galatians 6 says: 'Whatsoever a man sows, so shall he reap.' " When the news broke in the fall of 1974 of racial trouble in Baton Rouge, Louisiana, and the killing of Blacks by police there, one pastor offered prayers for the southern Blacks "suffering under the oppressor's yoke." On another occasion, prayers were requested for inmates of Walpole State Prison where there was turmoil. These church people are not ignorant of the world, nor do they ignore it. Lack of knowledge is not the problem. Further, social and political concerns are occasionally voiced in conventional terms within the church and specifically within the context of church services.

What does this evidence indicate about the churches' role within the wider social situation, that is, about their "politics"? If the church is reactionary, where have these progressive sentiments come from, and what is their significance?

It is worth emphasizing that the progressive political sentiments noted above are genuine, legitimate, and popular and are accepted by pastors and congregations as such. Within the question's context, the answer is threefold. First, the sermon statement calling upon Christ as the Healer of all ills is consistent with Pentecostal tradition. Among Pentecostals generally, and the Boston Mount Calvary churches in particular, this is theological orthodoxy. It is more than that, however; it is also an analytical statement about the human situation. It is a social as well as a theological statement. As social analysis, it uses a different vocabulary than conventional sociology and a grammar of causation that removes man from responsibility for the making and changing of history, placing that influence outside man. As theological language, it is rooted in the revivalist Holiness movement that swept rural America (particularly the South) after the Civil War and until the turn of the century. Coming at a time of rapidly changing social structure and of a shift from agriculture to industrial production as the dominant economic mode and at the very moment when man's capability for making and changing history was vastly increasing, this emphasis on a vision of God as the answer to all ills hastened the decline of the church's view of society into irrelevance. Moreover, such a vision has led to two distortions that persist in the Boston context. "One is the degeneration of the valid Christian belief that the life of faith produces transforming power into a naive judgment that the conversion experience will rectify all individual and social ills, and by itself humanize life. The second is the tendency to overlook persons and their needs unless they are 'prospects' for membership in the church—with the partial exception of the care provided for orphans, the sick, and the aged." [17] This perspective on the "world," which arose historically within a rural southern background, persists in an urban industrial setting in which it is not merely irrelevant but harmful in many ways.

Second, the population that espouses these beliefs and the vision of "God as the answer" is no longer in the South. These people are Black and experience a workaday world through that filter. Many of them are informed about events and have political concerns as well as a political consciousness appropriate to the information available to them. "Yes, I try to watch the news every night. Sometimes I read the paper and get frustrated over things political. I've become a concerned person. I've had problems with schools for my son, and this has made me more upset. I've had a friend go to prison for first degree murder. I visited him and saw what really went on. It really hits you when you become involved." On occasion they give vent to their concerns within the church. The dilemma they face is that their principal grammar of meaning and causation provides no tools by which any action they take in the secular political sphere can become religiously meaningful.

Third, the emphasis on individual salvation and on Christ as the Healer of all ills leads to a situation where "there is virtually no recognition of any responsibility (as Christians) to redeem the secular dimensions of community and national life";[18] thus, there is no religious construct really suitable for properly understanding and giving meaning to one's political concern.[19] What one gets is the translation of public issues into personal problems (if one may stand C. Wright Mills on his head) and the positing of a personal religious ethic as the solution to social and structural problems. The only time that a different response is likely is when a threat is posed to the church or its members.

17. Hill, *Southern Churches*, p. 198.
18. Ibid., p. 82.
19. Here the modernist attitude is crucial insofar as it is an attempt to transcend the personalist moral ethic and make secular political concerns and action meaningful in theological language.

In that event, a solution is usually fashioned outside the framework of religious meaning. The following case illustrates just such a threat and points to the irrelevance of this theological vision for coping effectively with the problem.

Practical Politics: A Case in Point

For some time, the Boston Redevelopment Authority (BRA) had wanted to appropriate the Alpha church property and raze the structure in order to carry out its plans for neighborhood renewal. It notified the pastor of its intentions, and after some dealing with BRA, he called a business meeting to inform the membership of the situation. He told the members of the history behind the BRA move, that it had wanted to take the property sometime previously but had been delayed and that this was only the most recent of a series of efforts on its part to take over the church. He showed a willingness to accept the BRA position on the matter and suggested that the membership begin canvassing possible sites to move to and/or build on. He asked for members' opinions, stating, "I feel that if it's the Lord's will, then they'll get it; if not, then their plans will be interrupted. They will give us someone to help us find a place. We can take the settlement they give us and make a down payment on a building and then renovate it. They will pay for us to move, and we can do that ourselves and add the money to it. If we get a mover, you know he's going to charge us what they give us." He also noted that whether the membership agreed or not, the BRA would take the property by right of eminent domain.

His remarks are enlightening in several ways: First, they evince a realistic understanding of the situation and an acceptance of the threatened loss of the church; second, the pastor's attitude conforms to the church's theological heritage. It signifies putting oneself totally into the hands of the Lord and acting on one's own behalf to conform oneself to the probable outcome, which is seen as the will of the Almighty.

The members' responses were equally instructive. With a single exception, they had no religious referent. The pastor's wife opened the discussion on a historical note, reminding the congregation that her family had had dealings with the BRA before and that they had literally been "taken." "It set us back twenty years." She counseled against being willing victims again. The rest of the membership took still stronger positions. It was suggested that another church (not in Mount Calvary) had fought the BRA successfully and that Alpha do the same, that otherwise they were not putting the Lord to the test; another member objected that the church was to be replaced with a playground and that the church was of more value and should not be given up; others rejected the proposal on the grounds that to move the church would inconvenience them, that the church was not a blight on the community, and that it was more than ever necessary to the health of the community with all the new housing being built. The basic thrust of sentiment was a rejection of the BRA takeover attempt and a willingness to fight. The pastor accepted the sentiments and agreed to inform the BRA of the membership's rejection of its offer.

A number of things stand out about this exchange: first, the willingness to accept events in the wider secular sphere as the "will of God"; second, the rejection of such events by the membership and the espousal of a strategy for dealing with the threat; third, and most interesting in light of our previous discussion, the almost complete absence of a religious rationale for the congregation's opposition. This is a cogent illustration of the threefold response to the question of the churches' role in the wider social situation. The pastor's initial sentiment, that suggested by tradition, was an acceptance of the chain of events and the consignment of the future "to the Lord in prayer." In the face of a direct personal threat, however, the members looked for a solution involving effective action on their own behalf; they did not adopt the quietist religious rationale available to them. Moreover, the solution agreed upon did not even invoke the religious framework within which they understood their lives. Their religious understanding was largely irrelevant to their effort to deal with a concrete social and political problem.[20] It may even

20. Hill, *Southern Churches*, pp. 82–83, 112–13.

have been harmful had they accepted the pastor's quietist proposal.

The political "blind spot" of the religious world view held by these Christians is clear in this instance. This is where quietism becomes manifest. It is not that these Christians are politically reactionary but rather that their religious world view gives them no handles with which to deal with secular events, other than prayerfully accepting them as the working out of God's plan. This is not simply an acceptance of events, however; it ignores responsibility for them. These people have no framework as Christians within which to understand their own political action. Thus, although they may act politically, they do so not as Christians or as a Christian community but simply as concerned individuals. Their action has no significance within the religious framework within which they understand their lives and the world. It is this dichotomy between accepting (or ignoring) events as the inevitable working out of God's plan and being unable to see that plan as meaning and justification for their own secular action that is to blame for the political quietism of these Boston congregations and of the churches of the Pentecostal–Holiness tradition generally.

This meeting and the dynamic involved were indeed extraordinary but not epiphenomenal. The state does not directly threaten every day, but were such situations a regular occurrence, the response illustrated above would still naturally follow. As noted earlier, the level of political awareness is relatively high, although there is not the sophistication or aggressive political self-consciousness that (presumably) characterizes some segments of the middle class. These Christians are not apolitical. It is, rather, the presumption that God's will determines history and the implicit sanction of "righteousness" this gives to the course of events and to the state that is to blame for the apolitical character of their behavior as Christians.[21]

21. This acceptance should also be seen against a historical framework of Christian quietism that de facto sanctions "things as they are" but in and of itself is neither acceptance nor rejection but an ignoring of the state and/or ongoing events as unimportant or meaningless within the

A note of explanation regarding the pastor's ready acceptance: He had suffered at the hands of the BRA before. Thus, his comment that the BRA would "get it anyway" is not simple defeatism but an accurate assessment of probabilities. It was also noted that "the pastor wants to build, period." The BRA challenge thus provided a convenient vehicle for upward ecclesiastical mobility.

In summary, then, except for the conference home that functions as a quasireligious community and some circumscribed extraecclesiastical association on the part of other members, the Mount Calvary churches in Boston have not been especially successful in grappling with the broader dimensions of community. They have been unable to extend the expression of their own religious community outside the boundaries of particular congregations. Thus, the church, despite its position as the major organizational affiliation in people's lives, does not provide a basis for a still broader communal association; rather, the wider communal expression of these people's lives is limited to the church.

It might be argued that church affiliation in fact constrains wider secular action. When such a challenge is carefully dealt with, however, it becomes clear that the church members' relation to the world is more problematic and, further, that the resolution of the problem is particular to the tradition from which Mount Calvary comes. The difficulty is not that religion is the opiate of the masses, deluding them and diverting them from knowing the world, but that, within their framework of essential meaning, namely, the religious world view, the stance it takes in relation to the world provides no way in which to understand either the phenomena of secular politics or their own political action in a religiously meaningful manner. It is not that these

---

reigning world view. In those cases where the religious authorities attained state power, politics and political questions were dealt with, but from within the religious frame of reference, for example, Calvin's Geneva, or New England's Protestant theocracy.

people do not understand the world. They do and, in some cases, act in it, but such action is not religiously meaningful either in individual terms (hence the problem at the personal level) or in corporate terms (hence the lack of political and community impact of these churches). They understand their corporate roles as limited to the "saving of souls," and the consequent definition of the world in terms of that salvific economy relieves the individual and the church as corporate body from responsibility for the reform of secular society. It is here that the differentiation within the church between traditionalists and modernists becomes significant, for one of the important problems with which the modernists are grappling is precisely this question of the relationship between the world and the church. They are seeking ways to make the secular world and the Christian's action within it meaningful in religious terms. Their success or failure will determine the future relevance of the church to the social problems of the community.

SEVEN

Summary

In retrospect, one is struck by the "normalcy" of these Boston congregations and their members. In many ways they are much like nonchurchgoers of the same socioeconomic status. More accurately, outside the church context, especially in the case of lower-class members, members of these Boston churches are similar to other churchgoing but non-Pentecostal individuals of similar socioeconomic status, more sober-minded than some but not necessarily most. The major difference between the two groups rests in the strong faith of the church members and the consequences it holds for their behavior, that is, the large amount of time spent in the performance of religious ritual and the leisure-time consequences of membership in a Pentecostal church that prohibits smoking, drinking, swearing, and so on.

The Mount Calvary churches emerge from our examination not as an exotic and peculiar cult but rather as a viable development, rooted in a particular moment of southern religious history and presenting an expression of that history in the present. These churches are a product of the Holiness–Pentecostal revival that spread in American Protestantism in the post–Civil War period and that had a particularly strong and lasting impact on southern Protestantism. The Holiness–Pentecostal churches, as part of the most radical evangelical wing of that southern tradition, emphasized the necessity of individual conversion, of "living holy," and of the rejection of the world and its wiles. The Mount Calvary Holy Church of America, Inc., was a beneficiary of a racial rupture within the ranks of this broad movement that led to the establishment of several specifically Negro churches. More specifically, the Mount Calvary Holy Church resulted from a split within the United Holy Church, which was itself a Negro spin-off from the Pentecostal Holiness Church widely established in North Carolina. It was from the United Holy Church that Bishop Bromfield Johnson broke and established the Mount Calvary Holy Church of America, Inc., in 1929. The major difference between the United Holy Church and the Mount Calvary Church was organizational—both churches were part of the same Holiness–Pentecostal tradition and shared the same world view and nearly identical ritual practices.

The churches that grew out of this tradition should be distinguished from the Pentecostal revival that is currently manifest within the Catholic church and "mainline" Protestant denominations. Although the religious impulse of the two movements is much the same, there is little organizational linkage between the older churches and the more recent Pentecostal development. More importantly, these movements exhibit different organizational dynamics. The original Holiness movement began within the established churches. When the Holiness people broke from the established churches and formed their own ecclesiastical structures, their membership became largely limited to the lower classes. Thus, the older Holiness and Pentecostal churches have a long-standing historical existence apart from the established churches, whereas the newer Pentecostals are remaining within their own mainline churches.

The older Pentecostal churches are differentiated among themselves along organizational and doctrinal lines although, among the Black churches, similarities outweigh differences. The organizational differences are the product of the different origins of the churches; they persist because of a tendency toward organizational self-preservation. (The trend in "the body of Christ," among Blacks, is still toward fragmented independence rather than organic reunion.) In practical terms, doctrinal differences are small and of decreasing import. There is one such distinction

between Holiness and Pentecostal; its basis is formally important, but it is less and less adverted to in people's consciousness.
It rests on a theological interpretation that, in addition to the
"second work of sanctification" decreed by the Holiness movement as necessary for salvation, there is a "third work" of the
Spirit that must be received "like in Acts 2:4"—namely, glossolalia—before one can become fully "justified" or "sanctified."
Thus, some churches such as the Church of God in Christ were
originally specifically Pentecostal; that is, they preached the necessity of speaking in tongues, whereas others remained simply
Holiness. In Boston, such doctrinal distinctions count for less and
less among Black "sanctified" churches, namely, those preaching
the necessity of "living holy" or living a "sanctified life." "It
doesn't matter who you are; if you're not holy, you can't make it
in. That's the part that counts. The name doesn't mean a thing.
It doesn't matter, man, nowadays. It used to be that way, but
even Baptists are 'pleading Holiness' now, and they'll tell you,
you've got to be holy." The Mount Calvary churches do not
preach the necessity of speaking in tongues as proof of the Spirit
baptism, nor do the members see such a distinction as important.
Further, members interchangeably describe themselves as Pentecostal or Holiness.

The Mount Calvary body claims "eighty churches in thirteen
states." The Boston churches were among the last established by
the founder, who died in 1972. They are therefore relatively
young in comparison with some other churches in the body, but
this is of less importance than their similarities to other Holiness–
Pentecostal churches, especially in Boston. Moreover, they have
been established long enough to demonstrate that they are not
fly-by-night affairs.

This study was specifically devoted not to the rise of the
Mount Calvary Holy Church of America, Inc., but to these three
Boston churches as representative of a type of religious phenomenon given inadequate scholarly attention and as examples of
current development among Black Pentecostal churches generally. Along these lines, the Boston Mount Calvary churches appear to be fairly representative. Two are small, like the majority

of Pentecostal churches among Blacks, and one is large; in Boston, there are several large Black Holiness–Pentecostal churches. The three churches differ among themselves as to demographic characteristics. The two smaller churches are basically lower class, whereas the larger church has a significant Black middle-class component. They are geographically scattered through the areas of Black settlement in Boston, although this makes little difference to their membership because Boston's poor public transportation requires that people travel by car or taxi, especially at night.

In considering in detail what constitutes church membership and what it is that church members do, our attention has focused on the ritual life of the church and the mechanics and dynamics of ritual performance. Indeed, liturgical performance was utilized as a central metaphor for the life of the church. In terms of the perceptions of both insiders and outsiders, ritual practice is one of the key components of church membership. Active members (upon whom this investigation focused) spent most of their time as "church members" engaged in ritual practice. The average active member is "in service" three times each week: Sundays (often all day) and Tuesday and Thursday evenings. In addition, members are expected to attend and support many special services and revivals, both in their own church and in neighboring churches. It is thus possible for the committed believer to spend all of his or her evenings "in the service of the Lord," if not at his or her own church, then in visiting other churches that are "in service."

Although extensive, the ritual life of the Mount Calvary churches is not overly complex. There is a basic set of components from which most services are constructed. Indeed, most services follow more or less the same format and are oriented around "revivifying the saints" and "saving the lost." There are, of course, other church activities, liturgical and otherwise, that serve other ends. Bible class is more or less straightforward instruction and guided reading in the Scriptures. Prayer meeting is generally a "round" in which individual members pray publicly for personal and public intentions. There are also Communion services, which are held at the discretion of the individual pastor, and occasional baptisms, ordinations, and christenings. These latter are less important to the ongoing life of the church and are in that sense secondary to the Sunday and other regular services and the frequent revivals.

Financial considerations are also involved in determining the frequency of services. Although it is not often openly acknowledged, services are held to meet the financial needs of an auxiliary or of the church sponsoring the service. Other churches are often invited to participate, and it is through this mechanism of frequent services and regular intervisitation that such large amounts are raised by such small groups of people. The three Boston Mount Calvary churches, totaling fewer than 200 members, raised $30,000 in 1972 and a similar amount in 1973. Assuming a total membership of 200, this averages $150 per member per year, and there are many who contribute more; the Alpha church, for example, with twelve adult members, raised $6,800 in 1972, which breaks down to more than $500 per member. The practice of tithing is one explanation for the high level of contributions; regular intervisitation is another, although members of Mount Calvary churches also visit and are a financial "blessing" to other churches. Given the amounts raised and the relatively small size of the congregations, it becomes apparent that financial support of the church can easily become a burden for those with families to support. Financial matters are thus a major source of grievance among members.

Not only is there a basic set of components from which most services are constructed, there are also a set of common and specified roles that people play in the ritual context. These elements of ritual practice are shared by a wide population, so that these components and roles are common not only to Mount Calvary churches but also to large numbers of people within the Holiness–Pentecostal tradition. Thus, whenever Mount Calvary folks and others gather in ecumenical fellowship—and they do so regularly—the ritual performance is commonly available to all, and all participate in its "production." On all occasions, ecumenical or otherwise, the ritual is performed smoothly; all un-

derstand what "score" from the ritual repertoire is being performed on that occasion and their own roles within it. This
contrasts with some descriptions of Black Holiness–Pentecostal
ritual observance as being less than orderly.

Given the amount of time devoted to it, it is obvious that ritual
is important for both the lives of the members and the life of the
church. As noted, the observance of religious ritual is one of the
main components of being "in the church." In turn, this practice
is not autotelic. Rather, it is grounded in a framework of meaning and belief that makes it meaningful and whose purposes it
serves. At the same time, the practice of ritual reifies or objectifies
the existence and reality of the beliefs. This is the "end" of
ritual activity and churchgoing. Given this reality, financial considerations remain secondary.

The church as an organized group exists to give flesh to, and
to be the embodiment of, the religious truths whose "real" existence the members presume. Thus, the church is both "that group
which engages in these liturgical activities together" and also
"that group which holds in common this set of religious under-
standings about the world, their place within it, and the Lord's
action within history." The relationship between the two is dialectical. Without the ritual enactment of the truths it holds dear,
the church would not exist in conventional terms; without the
beliefs to inform and give meaning to the ritual life, there would
be no point to its performance.

Two other important functions of ritual practice must be emphasized. First, in addition to giving flesh to the beliefs and
truths that the congregation holds dear, ritual serves to make real
the *subject* of those beliefs. Specifically, in the context of ritual
performance (although not limited to those occasions), there are
epiphanies and kairotic moments when the Lord, the Holy Spirit,
or the Spirit of God is made present within the community of
believers. The "Spirit falls" upon the faithful, and they experience His presence. It is not simply that ritual operates to reify the
principles of belief and to interpret the day-by-day experience of
believers in religious terms; equally importantly, in ritual "the
Word is made manifest and dwells among men." For the be-

liever, this is one of the central points of the service. Second, for the sinner and backslider, the ritual performance functions to bring about a confrontation between the sinner and the Almighty, often through the kairotic moments referred to above. In bringing about this confrontation, the evangelistic mission of the tradition from which these churches come is evident. It is this evangelizing effort that is one of the main religious functions of revivals. When this kairotic moment occurs, the church and minister have done their part; the sinner must confront the Almighty and himself, choosing either to abandon his life of sin and "claim his salvation" or to reject the Lord. Most southern Blacks were raised in a religious tradition that understood and utilized this approach to the Almighty, and sinners will often avoid a particular preacher to keep from being "convicted under his preaching."

The use of religious ritual as objectifying vehicle is not unique to the Mount Calvary churches or to Christianity. The importance of ritual practice in engendering the kairotic moment—that is, the intrusion and manifestation of the Transcendent within history—is, however, a central feature of the churches arising from the southern Holiness–Pentecostal tradition.

The focus on ritual performance as the life of the church has a number of other consequences. Ritual as major metaphor of the life of the church is also used to model forth the relationships that define the church as a social system. The status occupied within liturgical performance tends to be maintained outside it. Titles that obtain in church are also used in personal relations outside the church, even in the presence of nonmembers. This practice is not rigid, of course, and is dispensed with among those in the church who share a familial relationship. What is important here is that, although much circumscribed, the church as social world carries over its social system to the larger social world. Members of the church continue to relate to each other in ecclesiastical categories outside the church, one indication of the strength and tenacity of the church as a social system. Its impact and shape are felt and utilized by members outside its walls. It is thus not only a social world in and of itself (one of its sectarian characteristics) but a model for that wider social world in its ability to replace the everyday secular relationships and definitions between people. Its utility as a model of that wider world is limited, however, in the contemporary northern urban situation. In its southern past, the church was generally able to impose its view of the world upon the community. In the present situation, however, although it retains a degree of influence, it has lost its ideological and organizational hegemony over the lives of Blacks. Although able to put forward its world view and social system outside the walls of the church, this missionary effort is largely without community impact and is, moreover, often irrelevant to many of the problems and concerns that animate the wider Black community.

It is this irrelevance that must be kept in mind when considering the lack of social and political impact of churches from the southern Holiness–Pentecostal tradition and, in this case, the Boston Mount Calvary congregations. The question of the political significance of religious organization is usually dealt with under a quasi-Marxist rubric: Religion is reification and therefore not related to the "real" world; as such, it is harmful in that it diverts the masses' attention from the "real-world" source of their ills to a mythical system of causation and remedy. When applied to the Mount Calvary churches in Boston, this formulation is inadequate to the facts. It could be argued that the belief system that church members devote so much of their time to objectivating and invoking is illusory, but some church members spend time and energy thinking about and acting on "real" concerns—efforts that do not often yield fruit. Moreover, on occasion they voice their social and political concerns within the context of the church. It cannot be said, therefore, that they are concerned only with the mythical world of belief.

The issue of social and political concern must be formulated precisely to account for the relevant facts here. Given that church members have been concerned and involved in varying degrees with social and political matters outside the church and do occasionally give vent to these concerns within the context of the church, what then is the impact of the church on the world in these areas, and how is that impact to be understood, given the contemporary situation of these churches within a northern urban Black community? The answer is that the Black churches usually have little substantial impact upon the life of the communities within which they reside. This is true in terms of both the church as organization and the members as individuals. As noted before, the Pentecostal churches developed from a southern religious tradition that emphasized the life of Holiness, the evangelization of sinners, and the rejection of the world and its wiles—in short, an attempt to convert men to both the world view of the church and its social practice. Given the agrarian nature of southern life prior to the 1920s, such an approach to the world was viable and enjoyed some success, particularly among Blacks, because of the church's organizational and ideological hegemony. In a rural setting with a simplified agricultural order based on individual yeomanry among Whites and peasantry among Blacks, the personalist moral and social ethic of the southern church bore relation to the social facts of life. In the contemporary and northern urban setting, where existence is complex and influences on people's lives are much more earthbound than, for example, God's causing rain to fall, such a personalist ethos is clearly too simplistic for the actual social situation. However, the churches have not altered their ethos in any significant way to deal with the changed social situation. Without such alteration, their vision and their action in the world have little impact on questions of the moment, except when these questions happen to fit into the personalist ethos (thus, perhaps, the limited success of evangelical Christianity in reforming narcotics addicts). It must be kept in mind, though, that the churches' purpose is the mediation of an economy of salvation and not the secular political economy. It is no surprise, therefore, that the church lacks an adequate framework for understanding contemporary political and social life, which in turn makes it almost impossible for church members to undertake effective or systematic action in that world as Christians.

The church and its framework occupy a central place in the lives of church members, and it is through their church-derived meaning system that they understand the world and society. Because the church lacks an adequate perspective for dealing with the contemporary world, the member's faith is of little help in dealing with their concerns in this area. If they choose to act politically in civil society, they do so outside the framework of meaning their faith supplies. They act, therefore, not as Christians but as ordinary citizens of the appropriate socioeconomic status—as secular individuals. If they seek to act within the church and its framework, the only appropriate response to social problems is their consignment to the Lord in prayer. Thus, the church deals with those concerns, but in a way largely irrelevant to their solution (assuming a materialist view and ignoring the question of the efficacy of prayer and trust in the Lord as effective action in history). Thus, it is not simply that the church ignores the "real world" or is concerned with illusions but, more precisely, that the church's world view is largely irrelevant to current social problems and organization—thus the negligible impact of these churches on the life of the community.

Of importance particularly in the Boston situation is the effective political disenfranchisement of the Black population. Although Blacks make up a substantial segment of Boston's population (16.3 percent in 1970),[1] there are currently no Black elected officials within the city government. The present administration does not need Black political participation to govern and therefore has not encouraged it. Thus, on two counts, the church is "out of the action"; it lacks the history to make such activity an option in the present situation, and it feels no outside pressure (for example, from the city administration) to play such a role in the life of the community.

This is not to argue that a relevant approach to social problems is impossible. It does suggest, however, that, all things being equal, it is unlikely to develop in the foreseeable future. Nonetheless, elements of the theological tradition these churches share would make possible the formulation of a more relevant frame-

1. U.S. Department of Commerce, Bureau of the Census, *Statistical Abstract of the United States: 1972* (93rd ed.), table 22, p. 21.

work for political understanding and social action. An appropriate stimulus is necessary to foster such new thoughts, however, and such a stimulus is unlikely.

The Mount Calvary churches in Boston should thus be seen against a larger historical movement in American Protestantism, initially as a post–Civil War revival movement and then as a "left wing" of the southern Protestant tradition. As a form of religious organization and with regard to theological position, the Mount Calvary churches are by no means unique; they share features of ritual and belief with other Black Holiness and non-Holiness churches. Indeed, the southern evangelical tradition is common to southern Blacks and their churches. Thus, for southern Blacks, these churches are quite "normal," more rigorous in their ethics than the ordinary Baptist church but not therefore exotic or strange. These churches are all marked by the centrality of ritual performance in the lives of their members and the functions of that performance in uniting man with the Almighty. This focus is a central component of the heritage of the church and is also a mechanism for evangelization.

The emphasis on personal evangelization and the framework that informs it lead to an irrelevancy of political and social action on the part of both individuals as Christians and the churches themselves. This is a serious problem for which no immediate remedy is foreseen. In terms of its life and ends, however (and it must be remembered that secular and political influence is not the end of the church), these churches will continue their existence as long as there is a Black population for whom the world view these churches espouse is meaningful.

Epilogue

It has been some time since the research on which this book is based was completed. The fieldwork was done in Boston from fall 1971 through the spring of 1973, and the work began to take definite textual shape during the following year. Having finished the fieldwork, I left Boston and, despite the prayers and wishes of some church people and several attempts of my own, I have not managed to return for any extended period. Thus, I have not been involved on as intimate or continuing a basis with the members of Mount Calvary as they might have wished or as I would have liked.

I have, however, made periodic visits, which are never long enough; as I am told when I put in a long-overdue appearance, "Brother Paris, I thought you forgot how to come home." I have managed to keep in touch with a few folks in the church, courtesy of Ma Bell; and thus I have been kept up to date on old members, new members, various church feasts, and other pleasant events—as well as some that were not so pleasant. Such intermittent contact is by no means a substitute for close involvement, but distance has offered the advantage of perspective. Some things that were inchoate five years ago have become clearer. Moreover, I have a better sense of the developmental patterns that affect small Black Holiness and Pentecostal churches such as Mount Calvary.

Time has also offered a useful yardstick against which to measure a number of my original conclusions and ideas. Further, although I was sharply critical of the categories used in the literature to describe Pentecostal churches, the intervening history has worked transformations on some of my own. Part of the transformation has been produced by the regular movement of social process. When I first arrived in Boston (1971), for example, the South End where the Alpha church was located was still a neighborhood of the poor and the non-White. The housing stock was much deteriorated, there were large tracts of low-income public housing, and the Boston Redevelopment Authority (BRA) was still aggressively condemning and acquiring property for its own purposes. Interstate 95 was still being pushed as a means of reaming out unwanted residents and opening up the downtown central core to quick auto access from the south.

Since then, this field of social and structural forces has been almost completely reversed. The South End is now a trendy and up-scale area—albeit with a few remaining pockets of poor folks. Its proximity to downtown commercial development is an attraction for young White professionals employed in those office towers. The aged housing stock, long scorned in favor of suburban virtues, has reasserted its charms. Underneath the grit and neglect, gracious townhouse facades from the nineteenth century have begun to reappear. They offer more spacious quarters than comparable-cost housing in the suburbs, further increasing their appeal in this period of skyrocketing housing costs. A house on one such renovated block was bought for $8,000 in the mid-sixties. At that time its period charm and inherent livability were well hidden under layers of grime and years of abuse. Today it has definitely come up in the world. The woodwork and floors have been restored, the marks of abuse have been excised, brickwork has been pointed and masonry repaired, and it is selling for more than $150,000.

The neighborhood as a whole is undergoing this kind of physical transformation. The "original" inhabitants (those impoverished citizens who were abandoned like the neighborhood itself a few years ago) have been and continue to be dispersed along the front of gentrification. The Alpha church itself was a victim of this overall process while I lived in Boston, although, it was not gentrification but the BRA that was the agent of neighborhood change at that time. The BRA had been systematically acquiring titles and clearing property along the proposed right-of-way for I-95, and the process had an aura of routinized inevitability. There was a well-grounded sense of fatalism and an awareness of the futility of fighting City Hall. People were being systematically cleared out without recourse or much protest; their property was confiscated, and they themselves were forced to move elsewhere, generally farther to the south. This forced population movement has had long-term consequences for the receiving neighborhoods—heightened racial tensions, controversy over desegregation, shootings and killings in the high schools. Some of these consequences have been nationally visible, but they are beyond our concern here.

One set of consequences of this constellation of social forces is, however, directly relevant to our study. It has to do with the impact of this relentless redevelopment pressure on the physical and social structure of Boston's Black areas. When I was in Boston, the generally accepted zones of non-White settlement extended from the South End toward Forest Hills and Jamaica Plain on the south and west and into Mattapan and Dorchester on the east. The result of the forced migration has been to push the Black population as a whole farther south, much farther into Dorchester on the east and astride South Huntington Avenue on the west. Indeed, directly to the south, non-Whites (Blacks and Latins) have been moving into Hyde Park and other suburban areas that a few years ago were accepted as White preserves.

This development has important ramifications for the churches generally, and Mount Calvary exemplifies several of them. First of all, the relentless southward movement of the Boston ghetto changes the ecology not just of White neighborhoods on the frontiers but also of Black neighborhoods within the ghetto. As impoverished non-White areas are expropriated for urban redevelopment, the displaced residents increase pressure on housing in adjoining lower-income neighborhoods. Such pressure not only raises rents but abets the decline of these other areas by crowding "less desirable" tenants into them. Faced with this kind of encroachment, those non-Whites with the economic wherewithal move out in search of neighborhoods where the ambience remains desirable. Churches, as well as other community institutions, thus face a growing problem. First of all, insofar as their membership is local, the geographic dispersal of their members under such pressures threatens both the stability and the solvency of the churches. Conversely, if the congregation itself is forced to move, as in the case of the Alpha church, these problems are aggravated further, and the organization faces the additional problem of seeking out new (or at least newer) quarters with resources that have been severely depleted by the confiscatory nature of the BRA property condemnation process.

It so happened that the Alpha church successfully negotiated these large difficulties and was able to acquire another building (not formerly a church) farther to the south (lower Dorchester–Mattapan), which it converted into a church. Although this building was a considerable distance from the original church location, the congregation managed to stay together. This was especially significant because many of the members did not have cars and relied, therefore, on public transportation and other members to get to services. That the congregation sustained itself as it did was noteworthy because the added distance significantly increased travel time and generally made participation more difficult. It suggests, among other things, that the cohesiveness and bonds of loyalty of members to congregation are even greater than I originally suggested (cf. chapter 5).

The moving of the Alpha church raises another and more intriguing set of issues having to do with mobility. This congregation moved from an impoverished area to a much better one, closer to the "frontier" of Black settlement, an area of three-deckers and owner-occupied houses that is in marked contrast to the low-income projects and dilapidated houses and tenements characteristic of the original South End location. The residents of the new area are also better off, though it is difficult to specify the exact degree. Simply put, the building, its location, and the area generally are more substantial. There is not the decay and abandonment evident in the South End. The forced relocation in this case seems then to have resulted in "upward mobility." If I had originally encountered Alpha church in its new location, I would have considered it a higher-status organization than an equivalent congregation in the South End. The question arises, however: How does this move constitute "upward mobility"? The members (at least initially) are the same; their jobs have not improved; neither has their income or housing. The indebtedness of the membership, in fact, has increased (they received only $6,000 from the BRA and had to acquire a new building and finance extensive renovations). It would seem that appearances were misleading. The status of the congregation was still substantially the same. What changed was primarily the physical characteristics associated with this particular congregation. In retrospect, the earlier characterization of Alpha as a lower- or working-class congregation was accurate, and indeed the move was insufficient to lift this congregation typologically from that categorization. They now appear, however, to be upper-lower class, as opposed to the lower-class (lower-lower, middle-lower class?) category I would have placed them in earlier. The question persists: If, instead of a nonchurch structure that had to be renovated, they had acquired a bona fide church edifice—properly gray and stolid in appearance and with an appropriate patina of age—what difference would that have made? It seems to me that an investigator coming anew upon a congregation like Alpha in such quarters might have elevated them to a lower-middle-class ranking as opposed to an upper-lower. If so, this suggests that (*a*) our categorizing in this area has been more susceptible to accidental characteristics than formerly assumed; and (*b*) that historical background is an important complement to the categorizing process—another advantage of longitudinal analysis.

The point about the essential identity of the Alpha congregation in both settings having been made, it appears in fact that the forced change in location, by putting the congregation in a better area, gave it locational advantages and improved its appeal to a "better" class of potential members. Indeed, several people from the immediate vicinity have since joined, although the membership as a whole cannot really be considered a local or neighborhood one. In several cases, members have moved even farther from the current location than they were originally: One member now lives in Cambridge, to which the family moved from Allston—itself a good fifteen-minute drive from the original location and even farther from the present one. Another has moved to Brockton, some twenty-five miles to the south and really outside the local Boston area. It appears that several tendencies are at work simultaneously. The move has facilitated the church's appeal to a higher-status group of potential members, and some of those have been pulled in, thereby raising over time the social status of the congregation. At the same time, the currents of geographical dispersion are also affecting the church as some of the members "move up" to better residential circumstances, though not necessarily suburban ones in the conventional postwar bedroom-community sense.

The Boston Mount Calvary churches as a group have borne out my original perception of cyclical development. The Alpha congregation has increased significantly in size in the intervening years, whereas the Beta congregation has suffered a decline. Some of the reasons for Alpha's changed circumstances have been noted above. It can simply be reiterated that both the new location and the attractive renovation are "packaging" inducements to potential members. Church members would add also that "the Lord has blessed our work." Several younger, better-educated members have joined and actively participate in the church's life. Thus, it appears that the current Alpha congregation is as large, if not larger, than it has ever been under the current pastor. The members therefore have visible evidence that their work is prospering.

The Beta church, on the other hand, has seemingly suffered a loss in membership. When I was originally in Boston, this church had a large, active membership, several times the size of the other two congregations combined, and filled its building on Sunday mornings with 200–400 persons. It is still the largest congregation, but its membership has dropped precipitately. "I doubt if we get more than thirty, forty people of a Sunday any more," one member reported. There seem to be several reasons for this decline. First, this congregation was the main foundation in Boston—the headquarters church. As such, it had been Bishop

Johnson's home base, and he retained the nominal pastorate. The actual ongoing administration was handled by an assistant pastor, who was in point of fact the effective pastor because Bishop Johnson spent so much time traveling, preaching, and visiting other Mount Calvary churches. The assistant pastor, however, was scrupulous about maintaining the preeminence of Bishop Johnson as the pastor. The founder died unexpectedly during my first year in Boston (winter 1971–72), and the assistant pastor was subsequently made pastor in her own right. It is probable that a number of members felt a greater personal attachment to "Dad" Johnson, the founder, than to the institution he established or to the assistant pastor operating in his stead; and with his death they lost the link binding them to his church. If this be so, it was probably a gradual process, for I did not notice any rapid fall-off in attendance for this congregation while I was in Boston. Nevertheless, over several years, such a decline would have a significant impact.

Second, several structural factors might also have had an impact. Originally (1971) the Beta church was in a stable lower-middle-class neighborhood, near Grove Hall. It was composed primarily of one- and two-family homes on quiet tree-lined streets, with some apartment houses on the main thoroughfares. The redevelopment pressures that affected the Alpha congregation so directly had a spillover impact on the Beta church. Some of the people who were displaced from the South End moved into the apartments in the areas surrounding this church. This has had several results: increased population pressure on the housing stock; rising rents; housing deterioration, especially in the apartments due to decreased maintenance and the added abuse from vandals, teenagers, and others. The result was neighborhood decay and decline. Again, the better-off folks in the neighborhood left, opening up more spaces for "undesirables" to move in. The congregation's members are drawn from among the more stable if not better-off families, and if they leave the area, the membership goes down. The church is thus faced with the problem of proselytizing among an increasingly "undesirable" population. The Alpha church, by the way, has avoided this particular problem because its surrounding neighborhood has by and large not suffered this lower-lower-class pressure.

Further, the Beta church is at a locational disadvantage in that, although it is a substantial edifice, it is on a side street and not readily visible to passersby. Insofar as people become aware of a church by directly confronting it, or are attracted to it by seeing is members enter and exit on Sunday morning, Beta's side-street location mitigates against its gaining any significant number of members in this way. Unless one already knows about it, one is unlikely to be confronted by its presence, which makes the job of appealing to potential members more difficult.

Other factors, less structural perhaps, may also be contributing to the dilemmas besetting the Beta church. These are most often expressed in reference to congregational leadership. Dissatisfaction within Black congregations is often voiced in terms of grievances with the pastors. This does not mean that pastoral problems or differences are, in fact, the basis of the grievances —though they may well be. Rather, congregational leadership roles are, in effect, a lightning rod for dissatisfaction. Specifically in terms of the Beta congregation, several people reported dissatisfaction with the way things have gone in recent years. Little of what was mentioned was new or unique to Beta. Indeed, such complaints have been made about Alpha and Gamma, as well as about other Black churches in Boston. Basically, people complained that the Beta minister's preaching had become too worldly: "The saints don't get the food they need. ——— is up there talking about politics and telling married couples how to behave. Now that stuff is all right but not in church." Other complaints were in the same vein. At one level, as noted above, this kind of criticism is perennial and seems linked to the more personal basis of loyalty in a great many Black churches as opposed to White mainstream denominations. At another level, such complaints merit more than cursory attention because of their content (which was in fact specific to this case) and because of the developments within this congregation.

In regard to the complaints about the pastor, it is significant that they take on particular force and specificity at this time. The pastor had had aspirations for higher education, which had been long deferred due to the pressure of pastoral work and the larger organizational responsibilities she undertook on behalf of the national body. After the founder's death, however, she found a college program she could fit into her schedule; she has now received her bachelor of arts degree and is doing graduate work. The socializing experience of education has been well documented, and in this case there is no doubt that higher education affected this pastor's thinking and outlook. It may be some of these effects that the members are responding to in her pastoral ministry. If so, this raises some interesting questions. One can only speculate about them at this point, however. If the content of the Beta pastor's preaching has become "more worldly" in recent years, that is not necessarily a bad thing. From the point of view of the sociologist, it is self-evident that "putting all your trust in the Lord" will not by itself solve all problems. Indeed, as I argue in chapter 6, this means-end position regarding politics in southern fundamentalist Protestantism is an impediment to the churches' ability to confront the issues raised by the contemporary secular polis. Thus, it may be that the pastor, under the press of changed thinking, is attempting to address vital issues affecting the larger communal lives of her congregation. At the same time, members of her congregation may not want to hear something "new"—at least not in church—preferring instead the comfortable older pieties. What S. S. Hill says about White southern church folk applies equally well to these Boston Black congregations for the issues at hand:

In other words, when religion is defined as status, that is, how one stands before a morally requiring God, it follows that racial [and other social, I might add] concerns will not have more than approximate significance.

Despite their [minister's] courageous proclamation and example, when the evangelical concern shapes perceptions, this message is viewed as "tacked on," perhaps very important, but neither the central concern nor an organic by-product of the religious life.[1]

1. S. S. Hill et al., eds., *Religion and the Solid South* (Nashville: Abington Press, 1972), pp. 33-34.

This question has other sides, too, for churches rooted in this southern evangelical fundamentalist position have not been apolitical. Rather, their political stance has tended to be a conservative one; that is, their theological position has led them to support the existing political order and to be tenacious in support of the hegemonic position it has enforced on questions of public morals (alcohol availability and use, legalization of gambling, and so on). This suggests that part of the theological problem is finding appropriate forms within the prevailing theological position to encapsulate contemporary sociopolitical concerns. To paraphrase Malcom X: If ministers could clothe their social concerns in traditional religious language that their congregations could understand, they would then get the point. That this is not an insurmountable problem is evidenced by the effectiveness of Southern Christian Leadership Conference ministers in mobilizing their congregations during the era of the civil rights movement.

As far as the Beta congregation is concerned, it may well be that the discomfiture its members experience is caused by their objection to these "tacked-on" social concerns. When the pastor finds the hermeneutic keys to integrate these newer concerns within her conventional theological position, her members may no longer feel these new strands in her preaching as alien. Unfortunately, until then these concerns will continue to be a source of strain and estrangement. That this is not a trivial problem is indicated by some of the recent developments affecting the Beta congregation. Several members have transferred their congregational affiliation to the Alpha church; that is, they have maintained their Mount Calvary connection but transferred their congregational allegiance. The reasons may be complicated, but in this instance substantial disagreement with the Beta pastor on the part of some members is at least suggested.

It should be emphasized that this kind of decline is not unheard of. Just as the Alpha congregation exhibited a developmental cycle, so also does Beta and many non–Mount Calvary churches. Moreover, there are many reasons for this cyclical tendency other than those elaborated above. There are often disagreements between members and pastors over different kinds of issues: Members may object to what they feel are the pastor's excessive demands on their purses; indeed, the last several years have exacerbated this problem for Black religious organizations generally. Operating costs are outstripping revenues, putting increasing pressures on members for more and bigger contributions and more of their time. Conversely, members may feel that the pastor keeps too much power in his or her own hands or shares it only with a favored few or with his family, thereby denying others the opportunity for significant service. Of course, there are even more personal grievances. Members may dislike the pastor's wife, be scandalized by his or her private life, or decide that he has lost his "touch."

It is unclear in the Beta case which, if any, of these latter factors has played a role in the church's current difficulties. Although the complaints about preaching may indicate a more serious kind of dissatisfaction in addition to the rejection of modernizing influences discussed earlier, it is difficult to separate out the actual sources of discontent without close involvement. Further, as also noted above, such leadership-oriented grievances are recurrent and have been applied to other Mount Calvary Boston congregations in the past.

Although this developmental cycle is "normal" for many congregations, the actual course of its development in the Beta congregation is especially interesting. I noted earlier the potential for a split between the "modernists" and the "traditionalists" in the congregation. One might interpret Beta's problems as a case where the pastor herself became a modernist, so to speak, and has apparently run into difficulties with her more traditional congregation on that account. It is noteworthy, also, that several of those whom I had earlier described as modernists have since left the Beta congregation for other churches. It seems clear, however, that their break had a personal as well as a political dimension. It has been several years since they departed, and their departure seems to antedate the more recent problems. It appears, then, that my forecasting was correct in terms of the issues, if not the actual mechanics.

As for the Gamma congregation, it has also declined. Indeed, it has ceased functioning. This church, when I was in Boston, was the weakest of the three congregations, and apparently her ministerial responsibilities became too much for the aging pastor. There was no younger pastor available, the national organization had no one to assign to that church, and it was allowed to fold. Its members have dispersed to other churches.

Another area of church development, but one not linked to the developmental cycle discussed above, has to do with the churches' appeal to and recruitment of the offspring of the regular adult members. Here the results are decidedly mixed. A number of the teenagers whom I knew originally are no longer in attendance. The reasons vary: Some have moved away, some have fallen away, and others have joined other congregations. There does not appear to be a dominant factor or set of factors associated with this development. Of those who moved away, several went out of state—to go to school, for military service, to get married. Of these last, at least one has returned and again attends Mount Calvary, though on a lower level of participation than previously. A number of the teenage girls have become pregnant while still in school (before they reached eighteen). They did not marry and seem to have "dropped out" of the church. It does not appear that they were forced out. Mount Calvary and other churches sharing the same theological tradition do not permanently stigmatize a woman because she once had a child out of wedlock. Because of the kind of conversion experience emphasized, a woman who has "fallen away" can still claim or reclaim her salvation. Thus, for those who have fallen away and stayed away, it is more likely their own embarrassment, shame, or loss of belief that has prevented them from reconciling themselves to the church and its members.

Insofar as teenagers are concerned, one of the things that was most striking among the high school students was a conflict between the praxis of their elders and the habits of their extraecclesiastical peers, those at school and in the neighborhood. For a number of them, it was apparent that they would rather be "hanging out" with their peers than sitting in church. If they had not been compelled by parents, without a doubt they would have abandoned the church for other, more pleasurable activities, and many of them have done just that as age has enabled them to escape parental controls.

Another group was less emphatic about rejecting the ways of their elders. For these, the conflict between the sacred and the profane was much more internalized. Some have resolved the problem by falling away; a few have come around to fully embracing the church; and the remainder have fallen between the cracks, as it were—neither following the undisciplined habits of many of their high school peers nor adopting the "old-fashioned" church ways of their parents. At the time, all of these young people were negotiating the status passage from youth to adulthood, and it is probably within that problematic that their development can be most cogently explained. They have been dealing with the difficult racial situation in the Boston public schools, making career decisions, and learning about heterosexual relations in a permissive era when teenage socializing has been liberated from the limits imposed by parents and other adults. Thus, the "toll" in terms of pregnancies and muffed opportunities must to some extent be expected. That the world view postulated by Mount Calvary was unable to provide a better anchor for many of these young people is unfortunate, but at the same time it is symptomatic of the contemporary dilemma alluded to earlier. Moreover, this is by no means a problem confronting only religious institutions. As Jürgen Habermas makes clear, a crisis of legitimation besets virtually all authority in the West,[2] and what we witness among these young people in Boston is only a local manifestation of a much broader problem. I do not wish to downplay the significance of this failure of internal recruitment but rather to place it within a broader context of a general crisis of authority and thereby suggest that the problems faced by the Boston churches (in this vein) are in no way peculiar or particular. Interestingly enough, the recent growth of the Alpha congregation has tended to mask this problem for them. It is nonetheless a problem to which church elders are sensitive, and efforts have

2. Jürgen Habermas, *Legitimation Crisis* (Boston: Beacon Press, 1973).

been made to deal with it. Just how successful those efforts are and will be not only will affect the young people currently in the Junior Church but may determine the future prospects of the Mount Calvary organization as a whole.

In the long view, the analysis propagated herein has held up. The issues I flagged as key (such as internal recruitment and the traditionalist/modernist division) remain so. A few issues to which I paid less attention originally now impress me as almost as important as those I focused upon. The impact of public policy decisions on the morphology and well-being of Boston's Black population; structural and physical constraints on communal organizations, namely, rising maintenance and operating costs in the face of stagnant or even declining revenues due to the prolonged economic decline—all such structural factors I now see as important in their impact. Further, there is an incipient structural dilemma facing Mount Calvary and other Pentecostal–Holiness groups with aspirations to a larger collectivity. The problem, basically, is how to negotiate the transition from an individualized congregational focus to a supracongregational form—if you will, the shift from sect to denominational status. Part of the difficulty is paying the "cost" of the transition, not just the added expense of a superordinating layer of administration (which heretofore in Mount Calvary had been handled less formally by the Beta leadership with the occasional attentions and meeting of national boards and officers) but the diminution of local autonomy and its replacement by higher levels of centralized control. Up until the founder's passing, personal ties and loyalties overshadowed bureaucratized formalism in governing relations between local congregations and the national organization. Moreover it appeared that as long as "Dad's" charismatic presence was available it more than sufficed. The last decade, however, has forced some shifts. The death of the founder and the loss of his charisma, the straitened economic circumstances locally and nationwide and the consequences they have imposed on organizations, have increased the pressures on the Mount Calvary organization and heightened the necessity for organizational solutions to the fragmenting economic and social pressures. The church has made some moves to deal with these dilemmas, but it will be some time before one can judge the levels of success.

Such organizational transitions are a compound problem for churches like Mount Calvary, for they were often founded by strong individuals and are still run as individual congregations. The skills and interests of strong founders and builders are not infrequently at odds with the requirements of overarching organization, and Mount Calvary has had some difficulty in routinizing its founder's charisma and setting in place effective supracongregational machinery capable of shepherding the national organization through this next phase of its life.

Aside from these institutional and organizational issues, another factor that merits research attention is the way in which the overarching world views of fundamentalist and Holiness religion become integrated with the individual's personalized framework of meaning and understanding. The view developed implicitly here is that Pentecostal–Holiness religion is a variant of a larger southern evangelical and fundamentalist world view. Large numbers of persons of southern background are presocialized by the near hegemony of this ontological system in the South. Individuals, as believers, "plug in" to this framework of meaning in a conscious way and utilize its imperatives as rules, directives, and modes of interpretation for their own lives. There are conflicts between this view of the personal application of evangelical religion and the analyses predominant in the literature re adherents to such small religious "sects" and "cults." They have often been seen as psychologically and/or emotionally defective or as individuals requiring rigid institutional/emotional cocoons as a refuge from the wounds of day-to-day life in an oppressive society. I trust that my efforts herein offer a viable point of departure for coming to grips with a religious orientation that is by no means insignificant in contemporary society.

Appendix

The Method

Several possible sites were considered for field research for this project, and Boston was chosen partly on the basis of contacts unavailable elsewhere. The fieldwork was undertaken in Boston from fall 1971 through May 1973. It consisted mainly of attending church services and associating, insofar as was possible, with church members outside the liturgical context. A number of contacts were made initially in churches in the South End of Boston, but those for which I had prior introductions held the most promise. As a result, efforts in other churches were suspended, and I devoted my time exclusively to the Mount Calvary Holy Church. Initially, the Alpha church of this body seemed an excellent case for my hypotheses. (There are three churches or congregations associated with the Mount Calvary Holy Church of America, Inc., in Boston. It is not unusual to have a number of churches of the same organization in the same city—in Roxbury, for example, there is more than one Church of God in Christ and more than one United Holy Church—but the more common pattern seems to be a single church in a city, with churches spread over a large number of cities.) Alpha church was a "storefront" whose members were not indigenous to Boston.

This study was approached basically as an exercise in ethnomethodological fieldwork. I adopted and was adopted by the Alpha church, where I spent most of my time. It was helpful to have a "church home"; it made it easier for people to categorize me and both gave me a ready-made niche and obviated any hassles in establishing a primary identity as a researcher. In retrospect, it seems a good choice, for this church, although small in size, was of sufficient complexity to indicate the scope and function of the church organization. It was more representative of the conventional small Holiness church than the Beta church, which was physically larger and had substantially more members. The Beta church was also the national headquarters of the Mount Calvary body; this fact distinguished it from the other two churches in the study and set it apart from the ordinary "sanctified" churches in Boston. Personal factors also made Alpha a better choice than Beta. The Alpha pastor, although a member of the Mount Calvary body for less than ten years, was a bishop and the "state overseer" for Massachusetts. He possessed, moreover, in his prior church experience, a basis for comparison that longtime members lacked. In addition, most of the members of the Boston churches have come from other churches, so the Alpha and Gamma pastors were more representative of their memberships than the Beta pastor, whose association with Mount Calvary was almost lifelong. More important, Beta's pastor had long been charged with important business and official responsibilities within the church and would have been less sympathetic toward any developing views that she felt reflected unfavorably on the church. In that event, she might have tried to block my endeavors or unduly shape my perceptions. At any rate, my position as near member of the Alpha church gave me a readily available identity, an important factor because it eliminated much of the usual status ambiguity that participant observation often engenders. The situation was not all gain, however, for I felt constrained by the role in which people perceived me, in ways probably far beyond the actual constraints of the situation.

As nearly as possible, I was a "good" member of the church, although I did not formally join the body. Others perceived me as a member. I attended services like any other member and even led devotions on occasion. I contributed to the church financially, although I did not tithe. I accompanied the Alpha church on its frequent visitations to other churches. I became in all but formal affiliation a regular member of Alpha church. It was said, in fact: "Brother Paris sure is faithful. He's more faithful than some of our members." It might be argued that my regular attendance at the Alpha church limited the efficacy of my observations of other churches. In regard to the Beta church, I think such objections are unfounded, because I came to know several people from that church fairly well and sought to make up for any deficiencies in observation through formal interviews. The objection may have some validity for the Gamma church because that church was more or less inaccessible during the first year (it was difficult to reach via public transportation at night, and I did not have a car), and I formally interviewed only two members of that church. Nonetheless although my time was not equally divided among the three congregations, the knowledge gained through observation and secondhand information gave me an adequate understanding of the essential characteristics. Most importantly, the depth of involvement at the Alpha church corrected for deficiencies in breadth.

In addition to continuous fieldwork and observation, I collected twenty-seven taped interviews with church members. I had hoped to interview persons who had been in the church and then left, the "backsliders," but except for one case this was not possible. I was able to interview one other person who had been in the church and had left due to personal differences over financial and other church affairs. That person did not abandon the faith but transferred membership to a church with whose policies she felt more at ease (this is not an uncommon practice). With these two exceptions, interviewees were all active members of their respective congregations, the largest number being from the Beta church (which also had the largest membership). In addition, a few interviews were gathered primarily for historical material about the Boston churches. These interviews, together with the observational experience and the field notes, constituted the data base. The results were originally written up in Chicago during the summer of 1973, and the resulting manuscript underwent the first of several revisions during the fall of that year.

The Population

Because of scheduling problems and assorted mechanical and audio difficulties, several of the interviews are incomplete. Where important for the analysis, these differences in sample size are noted. The sample includes between one quarter and one third of the active members of the total Boston Mount Calvary population—namely, those who attended several times a week and supported the life of the church other than on Sundays only. In this respect, they are not representative of the total membership, which includes many more Sunday-only people than show up in the sample population. Pastors inveigh, however, against Sunday-only members as being "not really members of Mount Calvary," that is, less than completely committed. There was similar criticism of some of those interviewed: "They're not real members. . . . they've only been in the church a few years, they don't understand things." Such criticism was irrelevant for my purposes, because I was attempting not a historical study of the Mount Calvary "elect" but rather a study of these Boston churches as part of the larger group of Black Pentecostal churches, a phenomenon inadequately described in the literature. In these respects, the interviewees and their views appear fairly representative. Where necessary, the representativeness or lack thereof of the interviewed sample is noted.

The Boston churches are fairly young. There were attempts to establish Mount Calvary churches in Boston in the past, but these foundations (there were at least two) did not endure. The current churches, therefore, date from the early 1960s; in contrast, several churches in the national body date from the 1930s. Because of their youth, the Boston churches have no lifetime adult members indigenous to Boston. There are several people whose membership in the church antedates the establishment in Boston; they came to Boston, however, to assist in the establishment of churches there. The majority of church members have been members for less than ten years.

Few adult members are Boston natives. In the sample, six of twenty-nine are Boston-born, and the rest, with two exceptions, are from the South. Within the church population as a whole, the proportion of Boston-born members is less than the 20 percent in this sample, probably 10 percent or less. Church members followed the basic pattern of migration from the South characteristic of the general population with the majority being over age thirty-five. In terms of length of residence, only two in the sample have been in Boston for less than ten years, too small a number to be significant. There are indications, however, that substantial migration into metropolitan Boston continued through the sixties, contrary to popular belief. This trend has not been evidenced within the church. It seems that most of the church population consists of post–World War II migrants. In the sample, however, although half of the migrants fall into this group (post–World War II), there are twelve people who migrated to Boston after 1950 (the presumed cutoff for the postwar period). This group is younger than the postwar migrants; yet their commitment to the church and their faith seem as deep as that of their elders, although the younger group has more education.

One important inference to be drawn from the interviews is the rising socioeconomic status of the members of the churches. Although there is differentiation among the three congregations in this regard (the Beta church having a more substantial lower-middle-class segment, that is, people with lower-level white-collar and professional jobs, homeowners, and small-business people), the population as a whole has risen economically, beyond the level of their parents, substantially so in their own eyes. Excluding those whose parents were ministers, five of twenty-nine came from families that would be considered Black middle class. This seems to be a higher middle class percentage than in the total church population; it is a much higher percentage than for the two smaller churches (Alpha and Gamma), but, as noted, the Beta church has a middle-class element. Rising socio-economic status is not correlated with home ownership in the sample, however, as fourteen lived in their own homes in the South whereas only eight do so now. (This appears to be the effect of the greater difficulty of home ownership in the northern context.) Upward mobility is also apparent in terms of education. Only one member of the sample population had a parent with a college degree, whereas there are currently one nurse, two people with bachelors' degrees, and four others with college experience.

Another indicator that this is clearly no atomized, structureless ghetto population is the strength of the network of familial interconnection. With three exceptions, interviewees said they were "very close" or "close" to their families and reported frequent visits and telephone calls, and many trips to visit relatives in other cities and in the South. Church members generally have ties and family bonds in an extended network.

With few exceptions (four), members were not from a rural or agricultural background, an interesting aspect in the light of the conventional view of southern Blacks prior to 1950 as a rural peasantry. If that interpretation is correct, the present data suggest that those who became members of the church were better off economically than the mass of the Black population (or, possibly, that few former tenants and sharecroppers migrated to Boston), assuming, of course, that rural socioeconomic status was lower than urban status. If church members were a cut above the masses in socioeconomic status, a question is raised about the appeal of Pentecostal churches to the "downtrodden masses." Questions in this vein were put to several church members who reported that Mount Calvary churches in the South were, for the most part, established in towns and cities and not in rural districts and that, in fact, few farmers or sharecroppers were members of the southern churches. It may be simply that the location of the edifices dictated the demographics of the membership, but if this trait is persistent throughout the Mount Calvary churches, previous assumptions that such churches were filled with the "dregs of the population" need to be revised. The proportions of agricultural to urban/industrial background observed in the sample appear to be representative of the Boston Mount Calvary church population as a whole.

In terms of religious background, most of the present members of the entire church appear to have been formerly Baptists, although there are a few former Methodists and some with a

Holiness background. The sample interviewed gives a somewhat different picture: There are two Methodists, ten Baptists, and nine people of Holiness background. There are also a number of people of mixed religious background: Baptist and Holiness, Baptist and Catholic, Methodist and Holiness, and so on. The large number of former Baptists is to be expected because "most of them home folks is Baptist anyway . . . unless you go to different parts of North Carolina—we have Durham, Raleigh, Fayetteville Holiness churches—but all them little off-towns is Baptists." What is most significant about these figures is that all those interviewed were raised in the church, not Mount Calvary necessarily but some church. None came to the church in adult life on his own. This is not surprising when it is considered that Blacks have always had higher rates of religious participation than Whites. These figures suggest, however, that one must be a Christian first (and probably a southern Baptist as well) to be attracted to one of these Pentecostal churches (at least domestically—Pentecostal missionaries have had some success evangelizing Catholic foreign populations).

It also appears that there is a tie between "getting saved" and undergoing personal trauma, although I suspect that this is in part a "convention." A number of people spoke in this vein: "Well, I had just graduated, I had been under great mental strain, and things were happening slow for my profession, and it was back and forth, back and forth. I was seeking jobs, and I found I wasn't really using my talents, and I found myself getting deeper in debt, and I asked the Lord to show me the way and He did. Mount Calvary was the way. . . . I found relief, everything I've prayed for has always been answered. I wanted to be saved, I asked for it, and I got it." As is evident in this case, it is not necessary to have a dramatic experience of salvation, although Pentecostal churches are noted for the dramatic conversions often seen in revivals. Further, the experience of being saved is often separate from joining a church. The majority of those queried were either already saved when they joined or were saved after becoming members, but not necessarily at a Mount Calvary church or under the preaching of a Mount Calvary minister. It is in this light that the "defection" of members from other churches should be seen. Faith is not tied to a particular church or denomination, and members will leave one congregation for another for reasons having little to do with faith. Three of those queried joined the church because of contact with the founder, another because he was asked to serve as organist; but the greatest number joined because "I went there to visit and liked what I saw so I stayed."

People's faith is, however, very strong. The vast majority of those queried asserted that the church was either "the most important" thing in their lives or very important. Their heavy attendance, participation, and financial support point up its importance. The dynamic that appears to be at work is that there is a population of "true believers" linked to an institutional manifestation of faith that they find congenial ("You don't have to go to church to serve, but I believe in the coming together of believers"), and these people live out their lives of faith within this setting. One member stated:

If there were no ———, I'd go to another church. I would never stop going to church. In a church, you look to meet people, you look to hear the Word from the minister or whoever is bringing the Word, you look that you may go there and get a blessing. I always say that when I go to church I go to meet the Lord there. And I go looking for Him. Because when I'm here, people are making noise. Upstairs they're playing their old radio so loud. I say, "Let me get my hat and go to church where I can pray or think and hear the Word of God." It's just like honey. When you get to seeing and reading the things He say He'll do for you ... you go to church so much and you just live in church.

Selected Bibliography

Baldwin, James. *Go Tell It on the Mountain*. New York: Dial Press, 1963.

Banton, Michael, ed. *Anthropological Approaches to the Study of Religions*. New York: Praeger, 1966.

Becker, Howard S. *Sociological Work*. Chicago: Aldine Publishing Co., 1970.

Berger, Peter L. *The Noise of Solemn Assemblies*. Garden City, N.Y.: Doubleday and Co., Inc., 1961.

————. *The Sacred Canopy*. Garden City, N.Y.: Doubleday and Co. Inc., 1967.

Berger, Peter L., and Thomas Luckmann. *The Social Construction of Reality*. Garden City, N.Y.: Doubleday and Co. Inc., 1966.

Blackwell, James A. "A Comparative Study of Five Negro Store-Front Churches in Cleveland." M.A. thesis, Case Western Reserve University, 1949.

Blair, Thomas L. *Retreat to the Ghetto*. New York: Hill and Wang, 1977.

Botkin, B.A., ed. *Lay My Burden Down*. Chicago: University of Chicago Press, 1945.

Boyer, Paul. *Urban Masses and Moral Order*. Cambridge: Harvard University Press, 1978.

Bulletin American Council of Learned Societies, no. 32, September 1941.

Cone, James H. *The Spirituals and the Blues.* New York: Seabury Press, 1972.

Courlander, Harold. *Negro Folk Music, USA.* New York: Columbia University Press, 1963.

Davis, Arnor S. "The Pentecostal Movement in Black Christianity." *The Black Church* 2, no. 1 (1972).

Douglas, H. Paul. *Missionary Boston.* Massachusetts Council of Churches, Boston, Massachusetts, 1944.

Drake, St. Clair. *Churches and Voluntary Associations in the Chicago Negro Community.* W. P. A. Project Official Report 465-54-3-386. December 1940.

Drake, St. Clair, and Horace R. Cayton. *Black Metropolis: A Study of Negro Life in a Northern Community.* Rev. ed. New York: Harcourt, Brace & World, Inc., 1970.

Du Bois, W. E. B. *The Philadelphia Negro.* New York: Schocken Books, 1967.

Durkheim, Emile. *The Elementary Forms of the Religious Life.* Glencoe, Ill.: The Free Press, 1947.

Eddy, G. Norman. "Store-Front Religion." *Religion in Life* 28 (1958–59): 68–85.

Fauset, Arthur H. *Black Gods of the Metropolis.* Philadelphia: University of Pennsylvania Press, 1971.

Five Ethnic Groups in Boston: Blacks, Irish, Italians, Greeks and Puerto Ricans. A Joint Report by Action for the Boston Community Development and United Community Services of Metropolitan Boston. Boston, Mass., 1972.

Frank, Jerome, D. *Persuasion and Healing.* New York: Schocken Books, 1963.

Frazier, E. Franklin. *The Negro Church in America.* New York: Schocken Books, 1966.

——. *The Negro in the United States.* New York: Macmillan Publishing Company, 1957.

Frazier, Thomas R. "The Negro Church in America." Ph.D. dissertation, Union Theological Seminary, 1967.

Gerlach, Luther P., and Virginia H. Hine. *People, Power, and Change.* Indianapolis: Bobbs-Merrill Company, 1970.

Goffman, Erving. *The Presentation of Self in Everyday Life.* Garden City, N.Y.: Doubleday and Co., Inc., 1959.

Grey, Donald B. *Metropolitan Boston: Its Churches and Its People.* Massachusetts Council of Churches. Boston, Massachusetts, 1962.

Gutman, H. *The Black Family in Slavery and Freedom.* New York: Pantheon, 1976.

Habermas, Jürgen. *Legitimation Crisis.* Boston: Beacon Press, 1973.

Hannerz, Ulf. *Soulside.* New York: Columbia University Press, 1969.

Harrison, Ira E. *A Selected Annotated Bibliography on Store-Front Churches and Other Religious Writings.* Syracuse University Youth Development Center. Syracuse, New York, 1962.

Herberg, William. *Protestant, Catholic and Jew.* Garden City, N.Y.: Doubleday and Co., Inc., 1960.

Herskovits, Melville J. *The Myth of the Negro Past.* Boston: Beacon Press, 1958.

―――. *The New World Negro.* Edited by Frances S. Herskovits. Bloomington: University of Indiana Press, 1966.

Hill, Herbert, ed. *Soon One Morning.* New York: Alfred P. Knopf, 1963.

Hill, S.S. *Southern Churches in Crisis.* Boston: Beacon Press, 1966.

Hill, S.S., et al., eds. *Religion and the Solid South.* Nashville: Abington Press, 1972.

Hollenweger, Walter J. "Black Pentecostal Concept." *Concept,* Special Issue, June 1970.

International Sunday School Lessons. Philadelphia: Muhlenberg Press, 1954.

Jahn, Janhheinz. *Muntu.* New York: Grove Press, 1961.

Johnson, Charles S. *The Shadow of the Plantation.* Chicago: University of Chicago Press, 1934.

Lanternari, Vittorio. *The Religions of the Oppressed.* New York: New American Library, 1963.

Lomax, Allen. *Folk Song, USA.* New York: Duell, Sloan and Pearce, 1947.

McPherson, James R., et al. *Blacks in America.* Garden City, N.Y.: Doubleday and Co., Inc., 1972.

Mays, B.E. and J.W. Nicholson. *The Negro's Church.* New York: Arno Press, 1969.

Meier August and David Lewis. "History of the Negro Upper Class in Atlanta," *Journal of Negro Education* 28, 9.

Meriwether, Louise. *Daddy Was a Numbers Runner.* New York: Pyramid Press, 1961.

Nelson, H. M., R. L. Yokley, and A. K. Nelson, eds. *The Black Church in America.* New York: Basic Books, 1971.

Nichol, J. T. *Pentecostalism.* New York: Harper and Row, 1966.

Parsons, Talcott. *Religious Perspectives of College Teaching.* New Haven: Edward Hazen Foundation.

Phillips, Helen. "Shouting for the Lord." M. A. thesis, University of North Carolina, 1969.

Pope, Liston. *Millhands and Preachers.* New Haven: Yale University Press, 1942.

Raboteau, Albert. *Slave Religion.* New York: Oxford University Press, 1978.

Radin, Paul. *Primitive Religion.* New York: Viking Press, 1937.

Rawick, George. *Sundown to Sunup.* Westport, Conn.: Greenwood, 1972.

Reid, Ira de A. "Let Us Prey!" *Opportunity,* September 1926.

Robertson, Roland. *The Sociological Interpretation of Religion.* New York: Schocken, 1970.

Schneider, Louis, ed. *Religion, Culture and Society.* New York: John Wiley, 1964.

―――. *A Sociological Approach to Religion.* New York: John Wiley, 1970.

Schwartz, Gary. *Sect Ideologies and Social Status.* Chicago: University of Chicago Press, 1970.

Schwartz, J., and D. Prosser, ed. *Cities of the Garden State.* Dubuque, Iowa: Kendall/Hunt, 1977.

Sherrill, John L. *They Speak with Other Tongues.* New York: Pyramid-McGraw Hill Book Company, 1965.

Shibutani, Tamotsu, ed. *Human Nature and Collective Behavior: Papers in Honor of Herbert Blumer*. Englewood, N.J.: Prentice-Hall, 1970.

Spear, Allan H. *Black Chicago*. Chicago: University of Chicago Press, 1967.

Synan, Vinson. *The Holiness-Pentecostal Movement in the United States*. Grand Rapids, Mich.: W.B. Eerdmans, 1971.

Tavuchis, Nicholas. *Pastors and Immigrants*. The Hague: Martinus Nijhoff, 1963.

United Community Services of Metropolitan Boston. *Black and White in Boston*. Boston, Mass., 1968.

———. *Boston City: Some Population Characteristics in Four Areas*. Boston, Mass., 1968.

———. *Selected Social and Housing Characteristics for the Boston SMSA and the City of Boston*. Boston, Mass., 1961.

U.S. Dept. of Commerce, Bureau of the Census Statistical Abstract of the United States. 93rd. ed., 1972.

Valentine, Charles A. *Culture and Poverty*. Chicago: University of Chicago Press, 1968.

Wach, Joachim. *The Sociology of Religion*. Chicago: University of Chicago Press, 1968.

Washington, Joseph R., Jr. *Black Religion*. Boston: Beacon Press, 1964.

———. *Black Sects and Cults*. Garden City, N.J.: Doubleday and Co., Inc., 1973.

———. *The Politics of God*. Boston: Beacon Press, 1967.

Webb, Frank J. *The Garies and Their Friends*. New York: Arno Press, 1969.

Weber, Max. *The Sociology of Religion*. Boston: Beacon Press, 1964.

Williams, Lyle E., ed. *Light and Life*. Winona Lake, Ind.: Light and Life Press.

Williams, Melvin D. *Community in a Black Pentecostal Church*. Pittsburgh: University of Pittsburgh Press, 1974.

Wilmore, Gayraud S. *Black Religion and Black Radicalism*. Garden City, N.Y.: Doubleday and Co., Inc., 1973.

Wilson, Bryan. *Religion in Secular Society*. Baltimore: Penguin Books, Pelican edition, 1969.

————. *Sects and Society*. London: Heinemann, 1961.

————, ed. *Patterns of Sectarianism*. London: W. Heinemann Ltd., 1967.

Wood, W. W. *Culture and Personality Aspects of the Pente-Holiness Religion*. Paris: Mouton and Co., 1965.

Index

Library of Congress Cataloging in Publication Data
Paris, Arthur E., 1945–
Black Pentecostalism.
Bibliography: p.
Includes index.
1. Mt. Calvary Holy Church of America (Boston,
Mass.) 2. Afro-Americans—Massachusetts—Boston—
Religion. 3. Boston (Mass.)—Church history.
I. Title.
BX8770.P37   289.9   81-16169
ISBN 0-87023-353-X   AACR2